Jesus Is the Gift

The Spirituality of Advent & Christmas

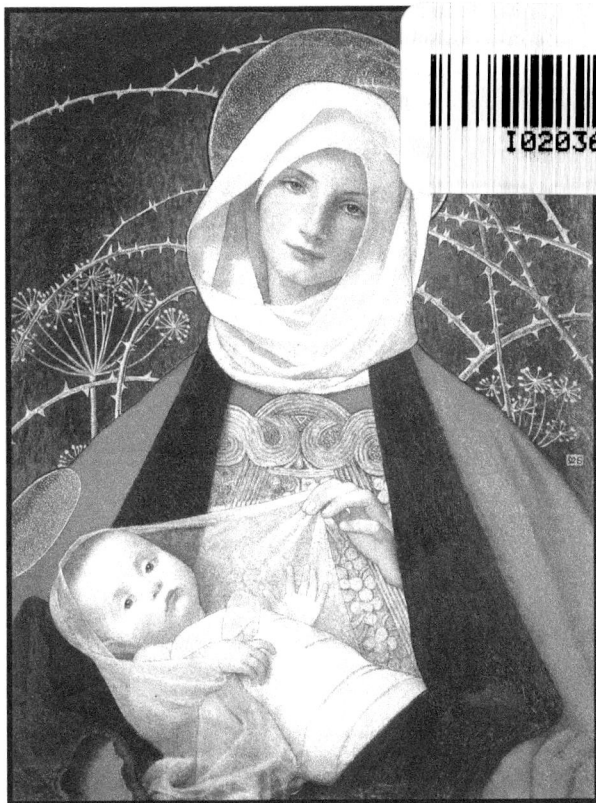

Jesus Is the Gift

The Spirituality of Advent & Christmas

REGIS J. FLAHERTY

EMMAUS
ROAD
PUBLISHING

Steubenville, Ohio
A Division of Catholics United for the Faith
www.emmausroad.org

Emmaus Road Publishing
827 North Fourth Street
Steubenville, Ohio 43952

Library of Congress Control Number: 2014952823
ISBN: 978-1-63446-001-9

Cover design and layout by
Theresa Westling

Cover artwork:
Madonna and Child, 1907-08; Stokes, Marianne (1855-1927)
©Wolverhampton Art Gallery, West Midlands, UK/Bridgeman Images

Imprimatur
Most Rev. David A. Zubik
Bishop of Pittsburgh
September 23, 2014

The *nihil obstat* and *imprimatur* are declarations that work is considered to be free from doctrinal or moral error. It is not implied that those who have granted the same agree with the content, opinions, or statements expressed.

*To my wife Libbie, my bride and
helpmate for thirty-nine years*

TABLE OF CONTENTS

FOREWORD

Every Advent, beginning in 2007, I prepared a talk on a theme of the season. I chose a character from Scripture as the uniting element in the presentation. I delivered these conferences not only at the retreat center where I live and work, but also at parishes and to various Catholic organizations. The chapters in this book are the development of my notes from those conferences. I offer them to you because some, who heard these talks, told me that they were helpful in their personal preparation for the coming of the Lord.

This book is not a Bible study, but spiritual reflections on the personages of Advent and Christmas and on what they teach us. My reflections certainly do not exhaust all that a person can learn from these biblical characters and themes.

I thank my wife Libbie, my youngest daughter Beverly Paul, and my friend and brother in Christ Richard Grebenc for the invaluable suggestions they provided in the development of the book. It is a far better product due to their help.

Whenever I put my fingers on the keyboard to work on this book, I want you to know that I asked our Lord to bless those who would eventually read its pages. May He, in His great mercy, use them to draw you to the true wonder and gift that is found in the liturgical seasons of Advent and Christmas.

Regis J. Flaherty
June 2014

INTRODUCTION
Preparing for the Coming of Jesus

Do you remember Christmas when you were a child? I recall the excitement that the approach of the holiday created in me. During the month of December, Christmas was never far from my thoughts. What gifts would I receive? With little resources, what present could I give to my mom and dad? Of course, the closer to December 25th, the more my excitement intensified.

On Christmas Day, we seven children would sit at the top of the steps on the second floor waiting until the entire family assembled. By that time we could hardly sit still. When my parents gave the okay, we would run down the stairs and into the dining room. There, at the place where we sat for every meal, we found treasures of our parents' love.

Then we had the opportunity to give to Mom and Dad our homemade gifts or hand-drawn certificates, in which we pledged extra work and service. My parents' appreciation for our meager offerings was always effusive and accompanied with hugs and kisses.

In my parents' home the focus was not only on the secular. They made sure that the spiritual aspects were front and center. The Catholic school I attended also helped me focus on the coming of Christ and the personal preparation that entailed. Mass in the festively decorated parish church and a visit to the manger were also causes for excitement and joy.

When I think of those childhood days, I can't help but recall the words of Jesus, "Truly, I say to you, unless you turn and become like children, you will never enter the kingdom of heaven" (Matthew 18:3).

We should find that childlike anticipation as we celebrate Advent and prepare for Christmas. The gifts of these liturgical seasons are of the greatest spiritual value. We receive the ultimate gift, Jesus, from our heavenly Father. We also can offer to God our seasonal gifts, meager in comparison with His, but accepted by Him nonetheless.

The Church gives us four weeks of Advent and encourages us to consider three epiphanies of Jesus.[1]

THE COMINGS OF THE LORD

First, we look back to the original event. We celebrate the birth of Jesus, God become man. Please pause for a moment on that thought. The words have become perhaps too familiar to us. We tend to lose the awe that should well up in us when we contemplate that God became man. We need to recapture the attitude of the child whose eyes are filled with wonder on Christmas morning. If God became incarnate, taking on flesh, history is forever changed. If He did not, Christians are to be pitied and rightly should be the laughing stock of twenty centuries (cf. 1 Corinthians 15:19).

That little baby in the crib is *God*. No other major religious leader has made this claim, except Jesus. This infant, whose birth we celebrate at Christmas, "is set for the rise and fall of many"

---

1. Epiphany is a feast of the Christmas season traditionally celebrated on January 6th. On the feast, we celebrate God revealing Himself to the Gentiles represented by the magi. In a more general sense, epiphany is the revelation of God to men. It is in this general sense that I use the term in this book. Advent is a term similar to epiphany. Advent is the four-week liturgical season devoted to preparation for Christmas. However, in a more general sense, Advent is the coming of God—in the person of Jesus—to men. It is in this general sense that I use the term.

(Luke 2:34). Christ's birth is the pivot of history—categorized by time before or after this event. His birth not only brings hope to those who live after the Nativity, it reaches back to Adam and Eve, expelled from the Garden of Eden, and to all people up to His birth. He is their hope as well. Consider, then, the micro effect. Salvation is offered to *you and me*. We are people of hope. We have a future. God became man for *my* salvation. That knowledge should make us incredibly thankful.

In Advent and Christmas we ask ourselves, "Do I thank God for the great gift of His birth that has changed history and opened heaven to me?"

IN THE HERE AND NOW

Secondly, Jesus is still with us in Word and Sacrament. Whenever we pick up the Scriptures and read them prayerfully, He speaks to us. In Baptism, He welcomes the recipient into the family of God and joins him or her to Himself as brother. When we go to Confession, He forgives us. For those in a sacramental marriage, His grace helps the couple to live their vocation. Most amazingly, He becomes truly present on our altars at Mass and resides in every tabernacle where the Blessed Sacrament is reserved.

Jesus is here now. We should explore how we can better love Jesus right now. In fact, you may want to imagine that you are holding the infant Jesus, looking at Him with love, and then ask Him how you can better please Him and love Him. Advent is a time to ask ourselves: "Do I love God? How do I show my love?"

ANTICIPATING A FINAL MEETING

Christmas is a vital link of a chain of events through which God brings us salvation—the Incarnation, the Nativity, Christ's life and teaching, the Last Supper, His Passion, death, Resurrection, and Ascension. One more event will complete the work of Jesus. That is His Second Coming at the end of time.

Returning in glory, He will judge the living and the dead. This Second Coming will be the culmination of the redemptive plan of God. Advent is a time to look forward to that future event. We don't know if He will return in five minutes or five thousand years. Either way we want to be prepared.

At that last coming of Jesus, there will be the General Judgment of all men and women of all time. We, as individuals, will also experience a Particular Judgment when we die.[2] At this meeting we will personally stand before the Just Judge.

Advent, then, is a time and opportunity to get ready—to ask: "Am I ready for Jesus to return in judgment? What do I need to do to get right with God?"

In summary, Advent and Christmas are liturgical seasons of grace.

- Time to thank God!
- Time to grow in our love of God!
- Time to get ready for His return!

HELPERS ON THE JOURNEY

In the chapters of this book, I'll present the key biblical figures of the Advent and Christmas story. They were the preparers for, and the witnesses of, the epiphany of Christ. They can teach us much that will help us during the seasons of Advent and Christmas, and throughout our lives.

---

2. "Judgment: The eternal retribution received by each soul at the moment of death, in accordance with that person's faith and works ('the particular judgment') (CCC 1021–1022). The 'Last Judgment'. . . . will coincide with the second coming of Christ in glory at the end of time, disclose good and evil, and reveal the meaning of salvation history (CCC 677–679, 1021, 1038)." United States Catholic Conference, "Glossary" to *Catechism of the Catholic Church* (Washington, DC: United States Catholic Conference, 2000). As of June 2014 available at http://www.usccb.org/beliefs-and-teachings/what-we-believe/catechism/catechism-of-the-catholic-church/epub/OEBPS/51-glossary.xhtml#glossary.

THE PREPARERS
Mary and John the Baptist

MARY
The Annunciation

When God banished Adam and Eve from the Garden of Eden, He gave a promise of salvation.[1] The Old Testament is the chronicle of the working out of that promise. It is the remote preparation—a long season of Advent—for the arrival of the Savior. God chose Abraham, whom St. Paul calls our father in faith,[2] to be the promise-bearer. Through the descendants of Abraham—Isaac, Jacob, Joseph, Moses, the Judges, David, and the Prophets—the plan of God unfolded. Then, "when the time had fully come, God sent forth his Son, born of woman, born under the law, to redeem those who were under the law, so that we might receive adoption as sons" (Galatians 4:4–5).

The final figures in the preparation of the unfolding plan of God are John the Baptist, whom we will consider in subsequent chapters, and Mary. With Mary, the long preparation that was the Old Covenant was drawing to its climax. In her, the promise enunciated in Genesis 3 finds its fulfillment. An angel visits her,

---

1. See Genesis 3:15.
2. See Romans 4:1–3.

calls her the favored one of God,[3] and tells her that she will be the mother of the long-awaited Savior.

> The angel Gabriel was sent from God to a town of Galilee called Nazareth, to a virgin betrothed to a man named Joseph, of the house of David, and the virgin's name was Mary. And coming to her, he said, "Hail, favored one! The Lord is with you." But she was greatly troubled at what was said and pondered what sort of greeting this might be. Then the angel said to her, "Do not be afraid, Mary, for you have found favor with God. Behold, you will conceive in your womb and bear a son, and you shall name him Jesus. He will be great and will be called Son of the Most High, and the Lord God will give him the throne of David his father, and he will rule over the house of Jacob forever, and of his kingdom there will be no end." (Luke 1:26–33, NAB)

This passage is rich in meaning, and meditating upon it can help us grow closer to God. Let's begin by considering the angel's first words, "Hail, favored one!" To be the favored one of Him who created the universe is the greatest privilege. It's far better than winning a billion dollars, better than being an Olympic gold medalist, better than being the most intelligent person in the world.

The angel's announcement informs Mary that she is in a special relationship with the King of the universe, the Ruler over all people and all history. Words like awesome, overwhelming, and breathtaking come to mind. Yet even these words are inadequate to describe the state of being "full of grace" (Luke 1:28).

---

3. See Luke 1:28. The New American Bible uses the phrase "favored one." The Revised Standard Version Catholic Edition uses "full of grace." Certainly there can be no greater favor bestowed upon a person than to be full of grace.

FAVORED—FAST FORWARD

The Church has taught us that Mary's favored position began at her conception:

> The most Blessed Virgin Mary, in the first instance of her conception, by a singular grace and privilege granted by Almighty God, in view of the merits of Jesus Christ, the Savior of the human race, was preserved free from all stain of original sin.[4]

Mary was indeed "full of grace"—the only daughter of Adam and Eve who could make that claim.

How did this favored status translate in the context of Mary's life? Let's fast forward from Mary's conception and briefly consider her life. At the time of the angel's visit, Mary was betrothed to Joseph and, after saying yes to God, is pregnant, but not by Joseph. It must have crossed her mind, "What will Joseph think? Do I tell him of this visit of an angel? How will he react?" Matthew tells us,

> Now the birth of Jesus Christ took place in this way. When his mother Mary had been betrothed to Joseph, before they came together she was found to be with child of the Holy Spirit; and her husband Joseph, being a just man and unwilling to put her to shame, resolved to send her away quietly. (Matthew 1:18–19)

Even though Joseph was a just and compassionate man—someone who would not subject Mary to public ridicule or to stoning that was the punishment prescribed in the Torah—nonetheless, she was in a precarious situation. The life of a single

---

4. Pius IX, Apostolic Constitution *Ineffabilis Deus*, December 8, 1854. As of May 2014 available at http://www.ewtn.com/library/papaldoc/p9ineff.htm.

mother would be most difficult. Fortunately, in a dream an angel sets Joseph straight.

Then, because of a government regulation, Mary must travel to another town when she is heavy with child. It's eighty miles from Nazareth to Bethlehem. Perhaps three days travel under good conditions. But of course, Mary is in the advanced stages of pregnancy. It could not have been a very comfortable trip.

She arrives in Bethlehem, and Joseph can't find a place that will take them in. Luke tells us, "She gave birth to her first-born son and wrapped him in swaddling cloths, and laid him in a manger, because there was no place for them in the inn" (Luke 2:7). Every mother and father wants the best for their child. If you are a parent, imagine how you would feel if you were in Mary's position. She had to place her Divine Son in a manger, a feeding trough for animals.

Shortly thereafter Joseph tells Mary that in a dream an angel has revealed to him that Herod is trying to kill the child Jesus. Therefore, they flee into Egypt, a journey of some 175 miles. Later, they had to make a return journey from Egypt to Nazareth.

Consider what we know of Mary's later life. She loses her twelve-year-old child while returning to Nazareth from Jerusalem, and must search for Him for three days. When He is an adult, she witnesses His public success but also His rejection, especially by the leaders of Israel. Eventually she watches her Son suffer a horrific death on a Cross. Who cannot be moved when seeing the Pieta—Jesus taken down from the Cross and placed into the lap of Mary?

FAVORED BUT NOT FREE FROM DIFFICULTIES

When we read that an angel addressed Mary as favored—full of grace—we should keep in mind the life that was ahead of her. God's favor did not translate into a life free from sorrow, difficulties, and trials. Quite the opposite. It brings to mind the famous prayer that was uttered by St. Teresa of Avila when she was thrown from her horse on a journey to a monastery: "Dear Lord, if this is how You treat Your friends, it is no wonder You have so few!"

Put yourself into Mary's position. Being the favored one and saying yes to God's request did not result in a trouble-free life. I don't know about you, but I'm pretty sure that I would be asking God, "What's up?" I would be tempted to anger, depression, doubt. I think we all would. When life doesn't seem "fair," many will say, "I have a right to be angry." We do not see this in Mary. I am sure she was tempted. Just because she was born without the consequences of original sin, including concupiscence,[5] doesn't mean she was not subject to temptations.

The only other woman born without sin was Eve, who lived in an idyllic world. Nonetheless, Satan successfully tempted her by sowing seeds of dissatisfaction in her mind. In essence, he tells her, "You know God isn't really that good to you. He will not let you eat of the fruit of the tree of the knowledge of good and evil. He's denying this to you in order to keep you from being more like Him." Eve bought the lie and sinned.

Mary could have done the same in the circumstances in which she found herself. She could have doubted God's favor due to all those situations of hardship—situations that did not confront Eve. Mary probably was tempted, but her response was different from Eve. Mary did not sin.

GOD IS WITH YOU

What was her secret and how can we learn it? Consider the second sentence uttered by the angel. After calling her the favored one, he says, "The Lord is with you." *That* is the key. *That* is the essence of favor. Mary knew that God was with her and she placed her trust in Him. No matter what the external circumstances, Mary's unshakable faith in God gave her

---

5. "Concupiscence: Human appetites or desires which remain disordered due to the temporal consequences of original sin, which remain even after Baptism and which produce an inclination to sin (CCC 1264, 1426, 2515)." United States Catholic Conference, "Glossary" to *Catechism of the Catholic Church*.

perspective and strength. In this we should imitate her. Consider the Catechism of the Catholic Church where we read: "By her complete adherence to the Father's will, to his Son's redemptive work, and to every prompting of the Holy Spirit, the Virgin Mary is the Church's model of faith and charity" (967). Adherence to God's will, obedience to God's directives, trust in His plan and in His love for her were the means through which Mary met the difficulties of life.

Ponder this prayer of St. John Eudes:

> O Blessed Heart [of Mary], so completely closed to the vanities of the earth and of self-interest that not one trace of them ever found place in you! Your confidence in God was equaled by your firm trust in divine bounty, and, fired with holy generosity, you never gave way before the obstacles raised by hell and the world to prevent you from advancing along the path of sacred love, but you always surmounted them with unremitting constancy and invincible strength.[6]

The source of Mary's unshakable faith in all circumstances and trials was the presence of the Lord with her. It should be the same with us. In Baptism we became children in the divine family—children of the Father in heaven and brother to Him who died on the Cross for us. Baptism has made an indelible mark on us.

> Incorporated into Christ by Baptism, the person baptized is configured to Christ. Baptism seals the Christian with the indelible spiritual mark (*character*) of his belonging to Christ. No sin can erase this mark, even if sin prevents Baptism from

---

6. Adapted from St. John Eudes, *Admirable Heart of Mary*, Part One, Chapter III. As of May 2014 the text is available at http://www.motherofallpeoples.com/2011/09/heart-of-mary-altar-of-sacrifice/.

bearing the fruits of salvation.[7] Given once for all, Baptism cannot be repeated. (CCC 1272)

No one can take away our divine filiation. We are children of God—period. Even when we seriously sin, the arms of our Father are always open to receive us, and we can repent and be forgiven through the Sacrament of Reconciliation. Mary's example calls us to embrace our status as a son or daughter of God. Indeed, we are favored ones.

When struggles come upon us, we must remember that God is with us. He is with you. He is with me. I am a favored one. You are favored ones. Seek Him! Trust Him! Take your eyes from the circumstances that plague you, look beyond the perceived realities of your life and see the greater reality. By Baptism we are children of God, no matter what may happen. If you are struggling with your spiritual vision, turn to Mary and see through her eyes and from her example that God is with you. Caryll Houselander writes,

> Our Lady said yes for the human race. Each one of us must echo that yes for our own lives.
>
> We are all asked if we will surrender what we are, our humanity, our flesh and blood, to the Holy Spirit and allow Christ to fill the emptiness formed by the particular shape of our life.
>
> The surrender that is asked of us includes complete and absolute trust; it must be like Our Lady's surrender, without condition and without reservation.[8]

Surely, Mary knew the story of Job who lost everything—family, possessions, health, friends. He lost everything *except God's favor*. Job was able to say, "Naked I came forth from my mother's womb,

---

7. Cf. *Rom* 8:29; Council of Trent (1547): DS 1609–1619.
8. Caryll Houselander, "Fiat" from *The Reed of God* (New York: Sheed and Ward, 1944). Reprinted by Ave Maria Press, Notre Dame, IN, 2006.

and naked shall I return; the LORD gave and the LORD has taken away; *blessed be the name of the LORD!*" (Job 1:21, emphasis added).

Job's friends said that his suffering was due to his sin. But Job learned that suffering is part of the human condition. And, what is more, suffering can be redemptive. What we do when we suffer, whom we believe, and how we respond make the difference. What do we do in the midst of trials? We turn our eyes to our Savior. Whom do we believe? Our Lord. How do we respond? We trust.

St. John Eudes, in the prayer that I quoted above, points out that the heart of Mary was closed off to the vanities of the world and to self-interest—two sources of temptation (the world and the flesh). Mary was invested not in the things of this world or in self-comfort but in God. She advanced "along the path of sacred love."

Love leads us to bear trials that we would otherwise avoid. Think of the sacrifices that a wife and mother will make for her husband and children. She dies to self to love and serve them. In fact, all of us must die to self in small matters so that we are ready to die in great matters—including martyrdom.

Mary was a daily martyr, dying to self and embracing God's will in everything, no matter how difficult. She was able to make those choices because she entrusted herself to God. Moreover, bearing those daily difficulties prepared her for the martyrdom that she shared with her Son as she stood at the foot of His Cross. Self-sacrifice and the love we call Charity[9] were the essences of Mary's Advent, her preparation for the birth, life, and death of the Christ, who was her Son.

We encounter difficulties in our lives (illnesses, financial set-backs, a child abandons the faith, death of a loved one, etc.). How will we respond? Like Mary? Will we entrust all that we encounter into God's hands and follow Him? Are we willing to work through all situations with God or will we try to handle everything with only natural lights and strength?

---

9. Charity is defined in the Glossary to The Catechism of the Catholic Church as follows: "The theological virtue by which we love God above all things for his own sake, and our neighbor as ourselves for the love of God (1822)."

St. Teresa of Avila who wrote, "We always find that those who walked closest to Christ were those who had to bear the greatest trials," also tells us,

Let nothing trouble you,
let nothing frighten you.
All things are passing;
God never changes.
Patience obtains all things.
He who possesses God lacks nothing:
God alone suffices.[10]

PONDERING

Tradition tells us that Mary was a girl of about fourteen or fifteen when the angel Gabriel visited her. Mary's initial response was a very human one—"she was greatly troubled." Yet, Mary does not lose her focus. She "ponders" the words of the angel. That pondering is a primary characteristic of Mary.[11] Pope Benedict XVI at a public catechesis said,

The stages in Mary's journey—from the home of Nazareth to that in Jerusalem, through the Cross where her Son entrusts to her the Apostle John—are marked by her ability to maintain a persevering atmosphere of recollection, so that she might ponder each event in the silence of her heart before God (cf. Luke 2:19–51) and in meditation before God, also see the will of God therein and be able to accept it interiorly.[12]

10. This prayer, called St. Teresa's Bookmark, is available as of May 2014 at https://www.ewtn.com/Devotionals/prayers/StTeresaofAvila.htm.

11. Luke 2:19, 51.

12. Pope Benedict XVI, "On the Praying Presence of Mary," March 14, 2012. Available as of June 2014 at http://www.zenit.org/en/articles/on-the-praying-presence-of-mary.

She reflects on what is spoken to her in the light of her relationship with God. This pondering speaks to the interior life of Mary. She could handle whatever she encountered exteriorly because interiorly she was united with God.

A QUESTION ASKED

Gabriel assures Mary saying, "Be not afraid." He then reveals the divine plan to her,

> Behold, you will conceive in your womb and bear a son, and you shall call his name Jesus.
>
> He will be great, and will be called the Son of the Most High;
> and the Lord God will give to him the throne of his father David,
> and he will reign over the house of Jacob for ever;
> and of his kingdom there will be no end. (Luke 1:31–33)

Although she was putting her trust in God, the angel's message did raise a question and she asks for clarification, "How can this be, since I have no relations with a man?" (Luke 1:34, NAB). This was not a lack of faith on Mary's part. On the contrary, she was seeking to understand precisely what God wanted.

This too should speak to us. We are not blind robots. We are God's children. We are to have faith that seeks understanding. That is the approach of Mary.

THREE QUALITIES IDENTIFIED

The author Federico Suarez finds three of Mary's virtues on display in her response. First, she accepted God's direction. He writes, "Because of her extraordinary and interior sensitivity to the . . . voice of God, she realized clearly that Gabriel was unfolding to her the Creator's plan for her."[13]

Second, she looks to God for the answer to her question. Her goal and motivation is to understand what God wants of her. Too often our response to confusion is hand wringing, frustration, and agitation, rather than going to God, seeking His plan, and trusting Him. Not so for Mary. She knew that the only answer to her perplexity would come from her Lord. She trusted that He would guide her.

Third, Mary does not fear. She knows that God is directing her and will provide for her. So, Mary's question is "simply asked for clarification, for in order to participate fully in the divine plan, she needed a clear knowledge of how she was to act, a clear idea of what she was to play."[14]

People who are not centered on God and His plan will respond differently. Their questions might be, "What will this cost me?" "What will other people think?" "How is this going to change my life?" "Can I have some time to think it over?"

A QUESTION ANSWERED &
A RESPONSE GIVEN

Gabriel provides the answer to Mary's question.

> The Holy Spirit will come upon you,
> and the power of the Most High will overshadow you;
> therefore the child to be born will be called holy,
> the Son of God. (Luke 1:35)

With this clarification, Mary gives her answer immediately: "*Fiat*"—"May it be done to me according to your word." Pause for a moment and take that in—a fourteen-year-old girl receiving a seemingly unbelievable message does not hesitate. If this is what God wants, then let it be!

---

13. Federico Suárez, *Mary of Nazareth* (New Rochelle, NY: Scepter Publishers, 2003), 10.
14. Suárez, *Mary of Nazareth*, 11.

Mary's response mirrors that of Jesus in the Garden Of Gethsemane, when He says to His Father, "Not my will, but yours, be done" (Luke 22:42). It also mirrors the words that we say in the Lord's Prayer. "Thy Kingdom come, thy will be done." If you want to imitate Mary, you can add "in me" to that sentence in the Our Father. Yet what do we really mean by those words? How often have we shown that we really didn't mean the radical trust and obedience for which those words call? If we pray the Our Father with the faith, hope, and love that Mary expressed, it should make us fall on our knees.

Her *fiat* to God's proposal effects the greatest of all miracles: the Word became flesh.

FINDING GOD'S WILL

Mary said "yes" without detailed knowledge of what lie ahead. The steps in God's plan were not revealed to her. His plan unfolded at His pace and required that Mary make conscious decisions one at a time—giving many fiats. It's no different for us. If we seek and listen, God will call us to a specific life-vocation: marriage, priesthood, consecrated life, or single.[15] However, the details of how our vocation will develop are not revealed. A "yes" to a life-vocation is only the introduction to a life-book with chapters to be written with the ink of daily living.

Occasionally people will say, "If I only knew then what I know now, I would have done things differently." But that is not the way God works. He intends an ongoing relationship with us. He doesn't send us on the road of life saying, "Good bye. I'll check back with you after you die." Instead, we embark on a faith journey that requires ongoing discernment and consequent submission to the directions of God.

A novel has not been written that can compare with the faith journey of any follower of Christ, whether for excitement, satisfaction, blessing, and yes, sorrow and pain. We need to continue

---

15. It is important to recognize that the single life is a vocation that can bear much fruit in the Body of Christ. I think this vocation is both underappreciated and under applied within the Body of Christ.

turning the pages and see what God calls us to this year, this month, this day, this moment. Although we might at times wish for more details, God will give us enough information (and grace) for the present situation.

Fortunately, we have the account of how Mary lived her vocation as our example. Mary's journey was unique, but each of us can say the same. God calls us each by name[16] to a great adventure that is custom-fit for us.

We don't want to lag behind our Lord or rush ahead of Him. For instance, I caution young couples who want to predetermine how many children they will have. A couple can't, or shouldn't, make that determination on their wedding day. It must unfold over time through the relationship of that small trinity—God, wife, husband. There is something healthy and life-giving about working through life one step at a time. Again to use the example of a married couple, in a good marriage they continue to grow in love as they travel life together. Trouble arrives only when they begin to think they know everything about the other person or when they stop striving to build a stronger relationship with their spouse and God.

Like a good marriage, so too our relationship with God.[17] We are in trouble if we do not continue to draw closer to Him. The greatest blessing in this life is to know and love our Lord. It is also preparation for an eternal relationship in the next life. We come to know Him through the unfolding of our lives and we grow to love our Lord more if we commit to walk with Him step by step.

Mary did just that. She was the handmaid of the Lord. In a sense, the Annunciation was a marriage (she is the spouse of the Holy Spirit). But Mary's relationship with God—Father, Son, and Holy Spirit—developed further over time as she faithfully walked with Him. It was an adventure that included joys and sorrows, questions and illuminations.

---

16. See John 10:14–15 and Isaiah 43:1–7.
17. See Ephesians 5:29–32.

Mary learned God's will by relating to Him. So must we. We must also seek His plan at all the stops along the way. That entails faithfulness in prayer, learning from our failures and mistakes, asking forgiveness as needed, and beginning anew.

In a catechesis delivered on March 14, 2012, Pope Benedict XVI said,

> The stages of Mary's journey . . . are marked by her ability to maintain a persevering atmosphere of recollection so that she might ponder each event in the silence of her heart before God (see Luke 2:19–51) and in meditation before God, also see the will of God therein and be able to accept it.[18]

WE REALLY WOULDN'T WANT IT ANY OTHER WAY

It is tempting to wish that God would reveal more of the details of our life in advance. Wouldn't it be easier to prepare if I knew one of my children would have a major illness or that my employment was going to end when I was fifty-five years old? Wouldn't it be better, before we were married, if I knew more about my spouse and about who she would become?

However, with a little reflection most people will agree that is not the best approach. Knowing the outcome of a game before starting takes away much of the enjoyment of the competition. Knowing everything about another person (which is impossible unless we are God) leads to boredom.

But the process of learning about each other can lead to greater joy and deeper love. It's a risk. Perhaps we won't like some of what we will discover in our spouse or in ourselves. We may not like what they become over time (or our spouse may not like what

---

18. Pope Benedict XVI, *A School of Prayer* (New Rochelle, NY: Scepter Publishers, 2012). As of May 2014 the catechesis is available at http://www.zenit.org/en/articles/on-the-praying-presence-of-mary.

we become!). Even with these concerns, the unfolding mysteries and nuances are worth the journey. Even if everything in life ends up being painful and troubling, the living of my life in an ongoing relationship with others and, in particular, with God is my highway to heaven, and that journey is always worthwhile!

It is a comfort to hear God's word through the mouth of Isaiah,

> I, the Lord your God,
>> hold your right hand;
> it is I who say to you, "Fear not,
>> I will help you." (41:13)

Knowing that God holds us allows us to accept that God does work for our good[19] and to face the unknowns of life with confidence.

NEED TO KNOW

So, God works on a need-to-know basis. As we said, it was so for His mother Mary and it is so for you and me. Mary's prayerful reflection, her pondering, would have been unnecessary if she knew all the details.

There is a wonderful story in *The Hiding Place* by Corrie Ten Boom that shows the insight and wisdom of her father. The ten-year-old Corrie asks him a question about sex and sin.

> He turned to look at me, as he always did when answering a question, but to my surprise he said nothing. At last he stood up, lifted his traveling case from the rack over our heads, and set it on the floor. "Will you carry it off the train, Corrie?" he said. "It's too heavy," I said. "Yes," he said. "And it would be a pretty poor father who would ask his little girl to carry such a load. It's the same

---

19. See Romans 8:38.

way, Corrie, with knowledge. Some knowledge is too heavy for children. When you are older and stronger you can bear it. For now you must trust me to carry it for you." And I was satisfied. More than satisfied—wonderfully at peace. There were answers to this and all my hard questions. For now I was content to leave them in my father's keeping.[20]

Corrie's father was mirroring the approach of our heavenly Father. There is a time that is right for us to know certain things and there are times when it would be inopportune. If God revealed the triumphs we will win by His grace over our life span, we might be tempted to pride. If He revealed all the sorrows and troubles that lay before us, we might be sorely tempted to despair.

In addition, God works with us on a need-to-know basis so that we will relate to Him. This is a preparation for the blessing of heaven where there will be no "events" but only true joy and overwhelming love based on a relationship with the Source of all that is good—a relationship we start in this world. Only in heaven will our sight be adjusted in a light that drives out all darkness. Now we see only in shadows. Then we will see Him face to face.[21] We get there holding His hand and walking one step at a time and listening to His direction. Mary, His mother and ours, will help us if we ask her.

FOR PERSONAL REFLECTION AND APPLICATION
- How do you respond to problems you face? Is your first response fear? Anger? Sadness? Mary's response was trust in God and turning to Him in prayer. Seek to develop the Marian approach in your life. Start by praying the Our Father with particular emphasis on "Thy will be done."

---

20. Available as of May 2013 at http://ecclesia.org/truth/corrie.html.
21. See 1 Corinthians 12:13.

• Are you anxious about the future? Meditate on the Scripture in Matthew,

> [Jesus told them] "Do not be anxious, saying, 'What shall we eat?' or 'What shall we drink?' or 'What shall we wear?' For the Gentiles seek all these things; and your heavenly Father knows that you need them all. But seek first his kingdom and his righteousness, and all these things shall be yours as well.
>
> "Therefore do not be anxious about tomorrow, for tomorrow will be anxious for itself. Let the day's own trouble be sufficient for the day." (Matthew 6.31–34)

JOHN THE BAPTIST
Leaping for Joy

The spiritual preparation of Advent includes self-examination, repentance, and acts of mortification. The effort of conversion—turning from sin to Jesus—requires work and a degree of suffering. Yet the Church also reminds us that joy and new life are on the horizon. Anticipation of the coming of Christ stirs us to better preparation and gives context and meaning to the penitential practices. We have a hope that is sure.[1] As the psalmist writes: "For [God's] anger is but for a moment, and his favor is for a lifetime. Weeping may last for the night, but joy comes with the morning" (Psalms 30:5). The sweetness of anticipation balances the struggles of preparation.

Twice during the liturgical year the priest wears rose-colored vestments at Mass, symbolizing rejoicing. One is *Laetare* Sunday in the middle of Lent and the other is *Gaudete* Sunday, the third Sunday of Advent. *Gaudete* Sunday celebrates the nearness of the Lord's arrival, and the joy and hope that accompanies that knowledge. On that particular Sunday, our focus turns from penance to

---

1. See 1 Timothy 4:6–10.

joy. *Gaudete*, Latin for rejoice, is the imperative form of that verb. It's a command like "Stop!" or "Run!" *Gaudete* is a directive to us: "Rejoice!"

The Catholic Encyclopedia states,

> Advent is [a season] of expectation and preparation for the Christmas feast as well as for the second coming of Christ, and the penitential exercises suitable to that spirit are thus on Gaudete Sunday suspended, . . . in order to symbolize that *joy* and gladness in the Promised Redemption which should *never be absent* from the heart of the faithful.[2]

JOHN THE BAPTIST

The Gospel readings on the second and third Sundays of Advent tell us of the work and preaching of John the Baptist. He prompts his hearers to prepare for the arrival of the long-awaited Messiah through repentance and personal conversion. Yet, John also encourages us to embrace joy. This encouragement to joy is a message that he delivers even before his birth.

Luke, in the first chapter of his Gospel, relates that an angel appears to the priest Zechariah, who will be the father of John the Baptist, while he is in the temple burning incense. Within the angel's message there are three words referring to joy. Let's review the angelic message with the goal of identifying some of the sources of joy.

The angel says to Zechariah,

> Do not be afraid, Zechari′ah, for your prayer is heard, and your wife Elizabeth will bear you a son, and you shall call his name John.
> And you will have *joy* and *gladness,*

---

2. See "Gaudete Sunday" in the Catholic Encyclopedia at http://www.newadvent.org/cathen/06394b.htm, emphasis added.

and many will *rejoice* at his birth;
for he will be great before the Lord,
and he shall drink no wine nor strong drink,
and he will be filled with the Holy Spirit,
even from his mother's womb.
And he will turn many of the sons of Israel to the
Lord their God,
and he will go before him in the spirit and power
of Eli′jah,
to turn the hearts of the fathers to the children,
and the disobedient to the wisdom of the just,
to make ready for the Lord a people prepared."
(Luke 1:13–17, emphasis added)

The angel's introductory words are "Be not afraid!" (v. 13). I think it is significant that the instruction, "Be not afraid," appears eighteen times in the four Gospels. It is a message we want to heed, because lack of fear, coupled with confidence in God, results in joy.

GOD HEARS OUR PRAYERS

What are the causes of this joy announced by the angel? They are many. First, there are very personal blessings that should evoke gladness in Zechariah. The heavenly messenger tells Zechariah that *God has heard his prayers.* Then, the angel tells him that his wife Elizabeth will conceive and bear a son. Zechariah is skeptical and tells the angel, "How shall I know this? For I am an old man, and my wife is advanced in years" (Luke 1:18).

It would seem that Gabriel heard the doubt in the priest's words, as he responds,

I am Gabriel, who stand in the presence of God;
and I was sent to speak to you, and to bring
you this good news. And behold, you will be
silent and unable to speak until the day that these

things come to pass, because you did not believe
my words, which will be fulfilled in their time."
(Luke 1:19–20)

I can empathize with Zechariah; perhaps you can too. I'm
sure he and Elizabeth had prayed many years for children, and
nothing happened. They had lived with the sadness of a married
couple unable to conceive. Now they are old, Elizabeth is past her
childbearing years, and an angel says that at this late date, at this
inopportune time, they will have a son. If God heard the couple's
prayers, why did He take so long to respond? Yes, we can understand Zechariah's doubt.

Yet the eyes of faith should see more. God's timing is not
always our timing. The plans that we think best are not always
so. That an answer to our prayer does not come at the time or
in the way we wish is not evidence that God does not hear. God
can work good in circumstances where we see no hope. He had
heard the couple's prayer. He answered it, and in a way they could
never have imagined. Their son, yet to be born, will be "great
before the Lord." The Holy Spirit will fill him from the time of
his conception, and he will demonstrate the Spirit's power in his
ministry. Through his work many of the sons of Israel will return
to the Lord their God. He will exercise his ministry "in the spirit
and power of Elijah." Divisions between fathers and sons will be
overcome. The disobedient will see the folly of their ways. He
will make the people ready for the coming of the Lord. In other
words, the child of Zechariah and Elizabeth will be a prophet and
the direct precursor of the Messiah.

The couple was looking for a child, a fruit of their marital
bond. Zechariah was frustrated at the seeming lack of response
from God. But God did hear the couple's prayer and He does respond. He gives them a son but He provides so much more—not
only for them but for all Israel.

God's answer to our prayers often exceeds our expectations
and has ramifications beyond our parochial concerns. But because

of our cloudy vision in this life,[3] we don't always perceive it. St. Paul tells us, "God is able to provide you with every blessing in abundance, so that you may always have enough of everything and may provide in abundance for every good work" (2 Corinthians 9:8). Consider also the words of Jesus.

> Ask, and it will be given you; seek, and you will find; knock, and it will be opened to you. For every one who asks receives, and he who seeks finds, and to him who knocks it will be opened. Or what man of you, if his son asks him for bread, will give him a stone? Or if he asks for a fish, will give him a serpent? If you then, who are evil, know how to give good gifts to your children, how much more will your Father who is in heaven give good things to those who ask him! (Matthew 7:7–11)

The knowledge that God hears our prayers is more than enough reason to rejoice.[4]

TWO VERY DIFFERENT RESPONSES

Before we examine more of the reasons for joy given by the angel to Zechariah, let's consider the priest's response to Gabriel and compare it to the response that Mary made to the same angel six months later.

There are parallels between the two messages and hearers. Gabriel brings them a message from God. In both instances he tells the hearer not to be afraid. Both messages announce a miraculous birth. Both Mary and Zechariah ask a question. What differs is the response of the hearer.

The Navarre commentary on the Gospel of Luke throws light on Zechariah's response.

---

3. See 1 Corinthians 13:12.
4. See the first point in "For Personal Reflection and Application" at the end of this chapter.

> Zechariah's incredulity and his sin lie not in his doubting that this message has come from God but in forgetting that God is almighty, and in thinking that he and Elizabeth are past having children. . . . When God asks us to take part in any undertaking we should rely on his omnipotence rather than our own meager resources.[5]

Later when Gabriel speaks to Mary, he tells her that her cousin Elizabeth "in her old age has also conceived a son; and this is the sixth month with her who was called barren. For *with God nothing will be impossible*" (Luke 1:36–37, emphasis added). That points directly to Zechariah's failure. He doubted that all things were possible for God. Nature dictated that a woman past childbearing age could not conceive, but God is Lord over nature, and it responds to His commands.

Mary's response is different from that of Zechariah. As we discussed in the last chapter, Mary expresses faith seeking understanding. The Ignatius Study Bible is helpful here.

> "How will this be?" Mary is not questioning God's ability to give her a son, but she is inquiring as to how such a plan will unfold. "I do not know man," which refers to Mary's *virginal* purity.[6]

JOY SPREAD FAR AND WIDE

As I mentioned above, God heard the prayer of Zechariah and Elizabeth, and He hears our prayers. Cause for joy, indeed! The angel's message tells Zechariah exactly what this good news means

5. José María Casciaro and a Committee of the Faculty of Theology, University of Navarre, trans. Brian McCarthy, *The Navarre Bible: St. Luke's Gospel* (Dublin, Ireland: Four Court Press, 1983), 34.

6. Scott Hahn and Curtis Mitch, *The Gospel of Luke: Commentary, Notes & Study Questions* (San Francisco, CA: Ignatius Press, 2001), 19, emphasis in the original. The Navarre Bible states, "How can this be?" expresses her readiness to obey the will of God even though at first sight it implied a contradiction: on one hand, she was convinced that God wished her to remain a virgin; on the other, here was God also announcing that she would become a mother. Casciaro, *Saint Luke's Gospel*, 39.

for the people of Israel and for the world: "Many will rejoice at his birth" (Luke 1:14). When John preaches as an adult, his message will challenge those who hear. It's also a challenging message for those of us in the twenty-first century. Conversion is difficult. Faithfulness is a struggle. Thinking and acting in godly ways that are opposed to the prevailing culture are not easy. Standing strong for the truth tests us. But there is joy because God is gracious. Even the name given to the boy by the angel is full of meaning; John = "Yahweh is gracious."

A VISIT FROM THE SAVIOR AND HIS MOTHER

Let's look at another passage from the first chapter of Luke's Gospel.

> In those days Mary arose and went with haste into the hill country, to a city of Judah, and she entered the house of Zechari´ah and greeted Elizabeth. And when Elizabeth heard the greeting of Mary, the babe leaped in her womb; and Elizabeth was filled with the Holy Spirit and she exclaimed with a loud cry, "Blessed are you among women, and blessed is the fruit of your womb! And why is this granted me, that the mother of my Lord should come to me? For behold, when the voice of your greeting came to my ears, the babe in my womb leaped for joy. And blessed is she who believed that there would be a fulfillment of what was spoken to her from the Lord." (1:39–45)

John, "filled with the Holy Spirit, even from his mother's womb" (Luke 1:15), directs his mother's attention to the primary source of joy in this world and the next. John leapt for joy in the womb because *Jesus was near.* Indeed, is that not what Advent is about? Jesus is near. We must talk about repentance, conversion, and other important aspects of John's message. But I think it best that we always start with joy. That is the way the angel began the announcement of the birth of John and that is John's wordless message to his mother (and to us). He whose mission was "to make ready for the Lord a people prepared" (Luke 1:17) begins his ministry proclaiming joy.

I appreciate the perspective of Father Thomas Dubay in his book *Authenticity.*

> The man who looks to the Lord radiates a joy from his inner encounter (Psalms 34:5). When God is near, good people sing for joy, they exult and rejoice (Psalms 68:3–4, 32). One must conclude that the normal human condition—it *is* normal to be close to God—is to experience an abiding joy.[7]

The Greek word for John's joyful leap could also be translated "skipped." Some commentators, therefore, say that John "danced in the womb"[8] of his mother Elizabeth.

Several psalms[9] speak of dancing, and it is always in connection with praising God. In addition, Miriam, prophetess and sister of Aaron, lead the women of Israel in dance when God rescued His people from slavery to Egypt. The most famous dancer in the Old Testament is David, who is credited with authoring many of the psalms. The story is in 2 Samuel.

> And David arose and went with all the people who were with him from Ba'ale-judah, to bring up from there the ark of God, which is called by the name of the Lord of hosts who sits enthroned

7. Thomas Dubay, S.M., *Authenticity: A Biblical Theology of Discernment* (Denville, NJ: Dimension Books, 1977), 161, emphasis in the original.
8. John Saward, *Redeemer in the Womb* (San Francisco: Ignatius Press, 1993), 26.
9. See Psalms 87, 149, and 150.

on the cherubim. . . . And David and all the house of Israel were making merry before the Lord with all their might, with songs and lyres and harps and tambourines and castanets and cymbals. . . .

And when those who bore the ark of the Lord had gone six paces, he sacrificed an ox and a fatling. And David danced before the Lord with all his might; and David was girded with a linen ephod. So David and all the house of Israel brought up the ark of the Lord with shouting, and with the sound of the horn. (2 Samuel 6:2–15)

What was the ark of the Covenant? It was the sign of God's presence with the people. It contained the staff of Aaron, a jar of manna (the bread that God bestowed on the Israelites in their journey to the Promised Land), and the tablets of the law (the Ten Commandments). David danced to acknowledge what God had done and to celebrate His ongoing presence with His people.

There are many parallels between David's dance and the dance of John the Baptist in the womb of Elizabeth.

- David danced before the ark because it signified God's presence. John danced because Mary is the Ark of the New Covenant—she carries the true presence of God within her.
- The original ark carried the manna, the bread that sustained the life of the Israelites. Mary carries the Bread of Life, which we continue to receive in the Eucharist.
- The original ark carried a rod, a sign of authority and the staff used by a shepherd to guide his sheep. Jesus is the Good Shepherd who will lead His people in the ways of righteousness.
- The tablets of the Law were the essence of the Old Covenant. Jesus brings the New Covenant into being.

APPROPRIATE EXPRESSION OF JOY

Even though David had many reasons to dance, not everyone shared his joy. David's behavior scandalized his wife Michal, who was a daughter of Saul, David's predecessor as King. She thought it was unseemly for David to dance with such enthusiasm in front of all the people. In fact, she said that he was acting "as one of the vulgar fellows" (2 Samuel 6:20). David rebukes her saying,

> It was before the Lord, who chose me above your father, and above all his house, to appoint me as prince over Israel, the people of the Lord—and I will make merry before the Lord. I will make myself yet more contemptible than this, and I will be abased in your eyes'" (2 Samuel 6:21–22).

It is appropriate to rejoice, to dance, in the presence of the Lord. We should follow the example of John in the womb of Elizabeth when he is near Jesus in the ark of the New Covenant. We should follow the example of David before the ark of the Old Covenant. It's even appropriate to act in a way that some would see as inappropriate. People will go to a football game with their face painted in the team colors, wearing outlandish apparel, and cheer at the top of their lungs for their favorite team. If those of this world are so focused on the things of this world, [10] don't we have a greater reason to rejoice, to dance, to act in a way that some would see as a little inappropriate as we prepare for the coming of the Lord? After all, we have the blessing of being in His presence, and is that not worthy of joyful exuberance?

Listen to what the adult John the Baptist has to say.

> He proclaimed: "One mightier than I is coming after me. I am not worthy to stoop and loosen the thongs of his sandals. I have baptized you with

---

10. See 1 John 2:15–17 and 1 Corinthians 7:31.

water; he will baptize you with the holy Spirit."
(Mark 1:7–8, NAB)

That's exciting stuff! That's far worthier of celebration than the sale on televisions or the colors of cell phones.

APPLICABLE TO YOU AND ME

Let's apply that concept of joy to the three aspects of preparation in Advent mentioned in the Introduction.

Our first Advent goal is to worthily celebrate the anniversary of His coming in history as God incarnate. That is a cause for joy. God became man to restore our relationship with God. The Jews were awaiting a Messiah, but few could have imagined that God *Himself* would come. What are some preparations we should embrace? Generosity, spreading the joy of the season by extra acts of service, and gift giving, especially in gift giving that is personal—giving myself to the other, as God gave Himself so personally to us—are good approaches. Our joy is a witness to the nearness of Christ.

When our children were young, my wife baked batches of cookies with their help. We then made individual plates of the treats for neighbors and arrive at their doorsteps singing carols while we delivered the cookies. As other members of the neighborhood heard of our tradition, they asked us to visit them as well. Soon we had to make our deliveries on multiple evenings because there were just too many deliveries for one night. To this day my grown children recall that tradition fondly, as do our former neighbors. It was an expression of our joy in celebrating the birth of Jesus.

Singing! We have some beautiful hymns that make wonderful prayers and sources of meditation. Share the gift of song with others and provide a musical offering to the Lord.

Gather with friends and family, and share the joy of the season. Two sisters, whom I know, have a list of favorite Christmas movies that emphasize the true meaning of the holiday. It's an annual ritual to watch them together.

After driving past three houses with Santa on the roof or in the yard, I am encouraged when I see the crèche with Mary, Joseph, and Jesus. For the last few years we have placed a wooden sleigh with one large gift inside it at the entrance to Gilmary Retreat Center. On that solitary package is written "Jesus is the Gift!" Even the modern world hasn't completely lost this element of joy, although many have lost the understanding of why we rejoice. Nonetheless, gift giving is a point of contact between the secular and the sacred, and therefore an opportunity for you and me to give witness to the true meaning of the season.

HE IS HERE NOW!

As mentioned earlier, the second epiphany we celebrate is His presence in our life now, especially in the Eucharist. When I was in grade school and high school, members of my family would go to Mass twice on Christmas. One parent would stay home with the youngest children and the others would go to midnight Mass. On Christmas Day the *entire* family would go to the liturgy. I can't ever remember considering that to be a hardship. In fact, I saw it as a privilege. It was a little "extreme" going to Mass twice on Christmas, but Jesus was there. It was our family "dance," if you will, before the Lord in the Eucharist.

When you receive Communion during Advent and Christmas, it might be profitable to think of those two arks—the ark of the Old Testament and Mary the Ark of the New Covenant—reminding yourself that you too are an ark of God when you receive Him in Holy Communion. In a unique and singular way, He is present in you and in those around you at Mass. It might not be appropriate to dance down the aisle at Mass, but it would be most appropriate to utter prayers and hymns from a heart full of joy—a heart that knows Jesus is near. In Advent, consider how you can "dance" in Christ's presence in the here and now, especially by visits to the Blessed Sacrament reserved in your nearby Catholic Church.

THE COMING JUDGMENT

Then there is that meeting with Jesus at the time of our death and at the end of the world. Death is a fearful event. We fear the possibility of physical pain and the grief of separation. These are very real concerns. In addition, many fear the unknown. That should not overwhelm us. God has revealed what awaits us, and if we die in the state of grace, we will enjoy the Beatific Vision[11]— intimacy with God that is beyond our present spiritual vision.[12] It is a sure bet because Jesus is our guarantor.

The secular view of hope is quite different. It is a hope that is far from sure. Someone hopes to win the lottery or to win a vacation to a place they always wanted to visit. Scripture gives us a different perspective. Consider the words of St. Paul and the author of Hebrews:

- We do not want you to be unaware, brothers, about those who have fallen asleep, so that you may not grieve like the rest, who have no hope. For if we believe that Jesus died and rose, so too will God, through Jesus, bring with him those who have fallen asleep. (1 Thessalonians 4:13)
- May the God of hope fill you with *all joy and peace* in believing, so that you may abound in hope by the power of the holy Spirit. (Romans 15:13, emphasis added)
- It was impossible for God to lie, we who have taken refuge might be strongly encouraged to hold fast to the hope that lies before us. This we have as an anchor of the soul, sure and firm, which reaches into the interior behind the veil. (Hebrews 6:17)
- Faith is the realization of what is hoped for and evidence of things not seen. (Hebrews 11:1)

---

11. The Glossary to CCC defines the Beatific Vision as follows: "The contemplation of God in heavenly glory, a gift of God which is a constitutive element of the happiness (or beatitude) of heaven (1028), (1720)."

12. I commend to your consideration my book, *Last Things First* (Huntington, IN: Our Sunday Visitor, 2005), which investigates in detail the life to come and how we prepare now.

Again, in the promises of God we find hope and in hope we find joy.

FRUITFUL OR STERILE

Finally, I want to point out one more noteworthy item in the story of David dancing before the Lord. As I mentioned, David's public joy, which he expressed in dance, scandalized his wife Michal. This story ends with the comment that Michal gave birth to no children. I think there is a truth here we must grasp. A joyless Catholic is a sterile Catholic.

This is particularly true in evangelization. Joy is contagious. It, along with love of the brethren,[13] should be a mark of both the Christian community and the individual. Many conversions start when a person sees the joy of a believer, especially in the midst of difficult situations, and wonders at its source.

At the end of the Year of Faith in November 2013, Pope Francis issued the first apostolic exhortation of his papacy, *Evangelii Gaudium*, "On the Proclamation of the Gospel in Today's World." He begins with this paragraph.

> The joy of the gospel fills the hearts and lives of all who encounter Jesus. Those who accept his offer of salvation are set free from sin, sorrow, inner emptiness and loneliness. With Christ joy is constantly born anew. In this Exhortation I wish to encourage the Christian faithful to embark upon a new chapter of evangelization marked by this joy.[14]

A joyful Catholic will be a fruitful Catholic. He or she will be a witness to a world where joy is in such short supply. When people ask why, we can provide the answer of John the Baptist—Jesus is near.

---

13. See John 13:34–35.

14. Pope Francis, On the Proclamation of the Gospel in Today's World *Evangelii Gaudium* (November 24, 2013), 1. As of May 2014 the text is available at http://w2.vatican.va/content/francesco/en/apost_exhortations/documents/papa-francesco_esortazione-ap_20131124_evangelii-gaudium.html.

St. Teresa of Ávila, the sixteenth-century Carmelite nun and reformer, said, "A sad nun is a bad nun." She also said, "I am more afraid of one unhappy sister than a crowd of evil spirits." We are not nuns, but St. Teresa's words apply to us as well. It is a worthy thought for Advent.

Whatever our "Advent," whether we are looking forward to Christmas, or to Mass, or to our death and judgment, if we are in the state of grace, we should rejoice.[15] Jesus is near!

FOR PERSONAL REFLECTION AND APPLICATION

- Read sections 2734 through 2737 in the Catechism. Consider the role of filial trust in your prayers. Are there obstacles you have erected making your prayers of petition disordered?
- God is gracious! Make a list of how He has been gracious to you. Rejoice in Him who has blessed you. Find the opportunity to tell someone about God's blessing and the joy therein.

---

15. Confession is the normal way to get into the state of grace if a person commits a mortal sin.

JOHN THE BAPTIST
Reasons for Joy
❦

As we discussed in the previous chapter, John the Baptist, while still in the womb of Elizabeth, points us to the primary reason for joy. *Jesus is near!* After feeling the movement of the infant in her womb, Elizabeth tells Mary, "At the moment the sound of your greeting reached my ears, the infant in my womb leaped for joy. Blessed are you who believed that what was spoken to you by the Lord would be fulfilled" (Luke 1:44–45, NAB).

Elizabeth's words point us to another reason to embrace joy. "What was spoken to you by the Lord would be fulfilled." Our God is a God of His word! He fulfilled what He had spoken to Mary. He will fulfill what He has spoken to you and me. Prayerfully consider the promises in these Scriptures:

- No temptation has overtaken you that is not common to man. God is faithful, and he will not let you be tempted beyond your strength, but with the temptation will also provide the way of escape, that you may be able to endure it. (1 Corinthians 10:13)

- In the world you have tribulation; but be of good cheer, I have overcome the world. (John 16:33)
- Jesus again said to them, . . . "I am the good shepherd, and I know mine and mine know me, just as the Father knows me and I know the Father; and I will lay down my life for the sheep." (John 10:7, 14–15)
- [Jesus said:] "Therefore I tell you, do not be anxious about your life, what you shall eat or what you shall drink, nor about your body, what you shall put on. Is not life more than food, and the body more than clothing? Look at the birds of the air: they neither sow nor reap nor gather into barns, and yet your heavenly Father feeds them. Are you not of more value than they? And which of you by being anxious can add one cubit to his span of life? And why are you anxious about clothing? Consider the lilies of the field, how they grow; they neither toil nor spin; yet I tell you, even Solomon in all his glory was not arrayed like one of these. But if God so clothes the grass of the field, which today is alive and tomorrow is thrown into the oven, will he not much more clothe you, O men of little faith? Therefore do not be anxious, saying, 'What shall we eat?' or 'What shall we drink?' or 'What shall we wear?' For the Gentiles seek all these things; and your heavenly Father knows that you need them all. But seek first his kingdom and his righteousness, and all these things shall be yours as well." (Matthew 6:25–33)
- I am with you always, to the close of the age. (Matthew 28:20)

These are only a few of the words of comfort and hope that God gives us. In fact, the entire Bible is the story of salvation history in which we see God protecting, guiding, and bringing men and women into union with Him. The saintly heroes of the Old and New Testaments did go through trials and, thank God, Scripture preserved both the blessings and the struggles. Seeing both gives us perspective as we go through difficult times in our own lives.

There is a story of a person who, as he was reading the Bible for the first time, was shocked by the trials, struggles, and persecution that God's followers had to endure. Then a friend suggested that he skip to the end—the Book of Revelation—and see there the victory that is in Christ. In the next to the last chapter of Revelation, the author writes:

> Then I saw a new heaven and a new earth; for the first heaven and the first earth had passed away, and the sea was no more. And I saw the holy city, new Jerusalem, coming down out of heaven from God, prepared as a bride adorned for her husband; and I heard a great voice from the throne saying, "Behold, the dwelling of God is with men. He will dwell with them, and they shall be his people, and God himself will be with them; he will wipe away every tear from their eyes, and death shall be no more, neither shall there be mourning nor crying nor pain any more, for the former things have passed away."
>
> And he who sat upon the throne said, "Behold, I make all things new." (Revelations 21:1–5)

When we accept the truth that God wins in the end and that He is with us now, we gain a clearer perspective on this earthly life, which at times seems like a "mourning and weeping in [a] valley of tears."[1] Regularly remind yourself: God is near and He keeps His word—both reasons for joy.

DIRECT FROM OUR MOTHER

Mary herself has some encouraging words. After Elizabeth speaks, Mary, echoing Hannah, proclaims the great psalm-prayer of the New Testament, which we call the Magnificat:

---

1. From the prayer "Hail, Holy Queen."

And Mary said,
"My soul magnifies the Lord,
and my spirit rejoices in God my Savior,
for he has regarded the low estate of his handmaiden.
For behold, henceforth all generations will call me
blessed;
for he who is mighty has done great things for me,
and holy is his name.
And his mercy is on those who fear him
from generation to generation.
He has shown strength with his arm,
he has scattered the proud in the imagination of their
hearts,
he has put down the mighty from their thrones,
and exalted those of low degree;
he has filled the hungry with good things,
and the rich he has sent empty away.
He has helped his servant Israel,
in remembrance of his mercy,
as he spoke to our fathers,
to Abraham and to his posterity for ever." (Luke 1:46–55)

Mary's Magnificat is a hymn of joyful thanks and praise. Those who pray the Liturgy of the Hours (the Breviary) recite it daily because it is as true for us as it was for Mary. Elizabeth heard these words and I'm guessing that John in her womb danced a little more!

WAIT A MINUTE!

At this point you may be saying, "Wait a minute, Regis. I believe what the Bible says but I'm not feeling joy." Later in this chapter, I'll enumerate some of the reasons we may not possess joy and some ways we can deal with that situation. First, however, I want to pause and address the concern that many people assert. "I don't feel joy" or, maybe, "I've never felt joy."

The English language muddles the definition of joy. Let me use another word for illustration. Love. People love God; they love their spouse; they love their pet; they love to watch television; and they love to eat hotdogs. Obviously, love has a slightly different meaning based on the context. Other languages have more words to cover those different meanings. For example, there are four words in Greek for love: *Eros, agape, filia,* and *storge.*

Our English word "joy" can have several meanings. Depending on the context, the more accurate word may be happiness, excitement, or pleasure. These words express feelings, and feelings are fleeting. At one moment I may feel happy, but something might happen to cause me to feel sad.

The joy Mary proclaims in the Magnificat and that caused John to leap in the womb is something more substantial, something that is meant to be lasting. Christian joy is a fruit of the Spirit. Paul in his letter to the Galatians lists the "fruits of the Spirit," which include "love, joy, peace, patience, kindness, goodness, faithfulness, gentleness, self-control" (Galatians 5:22–23).[2]

There is a passage in the Gospel of Luke that really brings out the meaning of true Christian joy. For someone who reads it for the first time, shock would be a likely response.

> Blessed are you when people hate you, and when they exclude you, revile you, and defame you on account of the Son of Man. Rejoice in that day and *leap for joy*, for surely your reward is great in heaven; for that is what their ancestors did to the prophets. (Luke 6:22–23, emphasis added)

Wow! If you hate, revile, and defame me, I'm probably not going to feel too happy, *but* I can still have joy. In fact, Jesus is telling us that we should leap for joy, just as John the Baptist had done in the womb.

---

2. The Vulgate translation also includes modesty and chastity.

Mary can help our understanding here. We speak of the Seven Sorrows (or Dolors) in the life of the Blessed Virgin Mary. They are:

1. The prophecy of Simeon. (Luke 2:34–35)
2. The Flight into Egypt. (Matthew 2:13)
3. The loss of the child Jesus in the temple. (Luke 2:43–45)
4. Mary meets Jesus on the way to Calvary.
5. Jesus dies on the Cross. (John 19:25)
6. The piercing of the side of Jesus, and Mary's receiving the body of Jesus in her arms. (Matthew 27:57–59)
7. The body of Jesus is placed in the tomb. (John 19:40–42)

We can be confident that Mary felt sorrow—the sorrow that perhaps only a mother can know—at each of these events. If she didn't feel sorrow, we would say she wasn't really human. Yet we can still say that she possessed Christian joy despite the depth of her sorrow. Why? Because Mary, among all created beings, possessed the virtues and fruits of the Holy Spirit fully. The Holy Spirit also offers the gift of joy to us and we, as Mary did, are to embrace and cultivate it in our lives.

Those of us who are parents know how a parent suffers when their child suffers. At the foot of the Cross, Mary experienced great sorrow but not despair. She was deeply wounded when she joined herself to her Son's suffering, yet she embodied hope.

THE EXAMPLE OF JESUS

Jesus also certainly experienced sorrow but always within the context of the joy in obeying His Father. Consider Hebrews 12, which is addressed to us:

> [Look] to Jesus the pioneer and perfecter of our faith, who for the joy that was set before him endured the cross, despising the shame, and is seated at the right hand of the throne of God.

> Consider him who endured from sinners such
> hostility against himself, so that you may not grow
> weary or fainthearted. (vs. 2–3)

Through God's grace it can be and should be so with us. We will experience sorrows, but they do not need to, nor should they, rob us of the fruit of joy. In any and all circumstances we are to be a people of hope who find joy because God is with us.

As mentioned, joy is a fruit. Think about fruit. The best fruit comes from trees with deep roots that soak up the nutrients from the soil. Since joy is a fruit of the Holy Spirit, it will grow when we have deep roots in the Holy Spirit. Firmly established in Him, we can withstand whatever comes against us—sorrows, pain, depression, difficulties, failures—and still say, "I know the joy of the Lord."

Trees with shallow roots are much more likely to be blown over when a tornado strikes, but those with deep roots can ride out the storm and remain standing. Certainly, the storms of life affect us. We do not escape unscathed, but we can continue to stand if we are rooted in the Holy Spirit.

Sorrow That Draws Us Close to God

There can be a sorrow that comes from the devil, but there is also sorrow that leads us closer to God. Mary, who was so close to her Son from the moment of His conception, drew even closer by sharing in His suffering. We too come closer to God when we join our suffering with His. The suffering of Jesus was, and is, redemptive. Christ's death means life for us.

Our dying to self and embracing Christ and His will not only mean deeper life for us in Christ, but also the opportunity to bless others. Isn't that the essence of joy? True joy does not come from what we have but from who we are. To suffer for the one you love is a struggle, but ultimately it is a joy to share in the burdens of the beloved—especially when it is self-sacrificial and when it benefits and blesses the other. For example, the happiest marriages are not those in which the husband and wife are striving to get their own needs met. The happiest couples are those who practice committed self-sacrificial love.

JOY AND DEPRESSION?

Again, I need to pause and explore another concern that arises. Many people suffer from depression, sometimes severe depression. They, and those who love them, will be tempted to think they cannot possess this virtue of joy. There are many contributing factors to depression, but, in and of itself, depression cannot rob the Catholic of the virtue of joy, even when it denies the person the feeling of joy.[3]

There have been saints and deeply religious people who struggled with depression and melancholia:[4] Mother Teresa of Calcutta, St. Elizabeth Anne Seton, the poet Gerard Manley Hopkins who wrote, "The world is charged with the grandeur of God" (someone lacking joy could not write the poetry that Hopkins did), and St. Jane de Chantal, "who struggled with depression-like feelings for forty years."[5]

Aaron Kheriaty in *Catholic Guide to Depression* states:

> Throughout history, many saints and people of heroic virtue suffered from mental illness of one sort or another. . . . If the saints, the men and women *closest* to God who were *exemplary* in their faith and good works, experienced profound sorrow and even periods of depression, then it

3. On this important topic I highly recommend Aaron Kheriaty, MD with Fr. John Cihak, STD, *The Catholic Guide to Depression: How the Saints, the Sacraments, and Psychiatry Can Help You Break Its Grip and Find Happiness Again* (Manchester, NH: Sophia Institute Press, 2012), hereafter referred to as Catholic Guide in the notes.

4. Melancholia was often the term used for depression like symptoms before the term "depression" was widely used.

5. See Bert Ghezzi at http://www.bertghezzi.com/id18.html). Ghezzi points to factors that helped the saint deal with depression. Trust the Lord; maintain wholesome relationships with friends; refuse to fear or engage troubling thoughts; divert attention from your problems by reaching out to others. Ghezzi also adds, "This prescription is not a cure-all. And it is not a substitute for professional help."

certainly follows faith alone does not inoculate the believer against this affliction.[6]

Christian joy does not preclude the emotion or feeling of sorrow or sadness, or even depression. All of us, who live in the post Garden of Eden world, will know sorrow at times. It has been so since the beginning when Adam and Eve lost paradise. What sorrow they must have felt, but God did not abandon them and, because God continued to love them, they could still embrace joy. So the virtue of joy is different from the feeling of joy. The first can be with us through all circumstances, while the second will come and go.

Kheriaty writes, "Sorrow will be present in the life of every believer, but it is something that is used by God to bring the disciple into closer union with him."[7] No matter how deep the sorrow or cutting the pain, if it brings us closer to Jesus, we find joy. Kheriaty adds, "In Christ, one has existential joy amid the darkest hours of life."[8]

Not only people with depression but also those with other deep-seated struggles can demonstrate the fruit of joy. Consider the person who is severely handicapped, the person who has a homosexual orientation and tries to live chastely, the person who is divorced and lonely, and you can add many others who have various struggles and sufferings. If God is true to His promises, joy can be a part of the lives of all of His followers.

The Value of Sorrow and Suffering

In addition, to experience sorrow or sadness as an emotion is not always a bad thing. Scripture points out that there is "a time to weep, and a time to laugh; a time to mourn, and a time to dance" (Ecclesiastes 3:4). It is appropriate and important for us to empathize with others. St. Paul tells us to "rejoice with those who rejoice, weep with those who weep" (Romans 12:15).

---

6. Kheriaty, *Catholic Guide*, xxviii.
7. Ibid., 53.
8. Ibid., 55.

Jesus wept at the grave of Lazarus when He knew that He could and would raise him from the dead.[9] I think the above Scripture verse from Romans is the key to understanding the reason. Mary and Martha were in sorrow over the death of their dear brother, and Jesus empathized with them. He literally wept with them.

I know people, and you may as well, who have experienced bouts of depression, sometimes severe, but have never lost hope and trust in God. One woman that I know is able to help others in a way that those who haven't experienced depression ever could, because of what she suffered. She is able to convey hope and trust in God to a person who is struggling with depression because she knows the struggle personally.

Indeed our sorrows should lead us not only to empathize but also to encourage others.

Remember that we live in a fallen world. We will only experience the new heavens and new earth after Jesus returns and His kingdom is fully established.[10] There is much in this fallen world that will cause us to experience misery and woe. Sin, natural disasters, sickness—all cause sadness in us. But sorrow, as with any other emotion, is not good or bad in and of itself. It is what we do with it that makes a difference

Think of anger. One person gets angry at an injustice and kills someone. Another gets angry over injustice and then works to create a more just society, perhaps by political action or by involvement in a charitable organization. Paul puts anger in perspective when he writes, "Therefore, putting away falsehood, speak the truth, each one to his neighbor, for we are members one of another. Be angry but do not sin" (Ephesians 4:25–26, NAB). Falsehood should make us angry, but we should not let that anger lead us to sin. Instead, we need to use that anger to produce good.

Similarly, one person experiences profound sorrow and is led to despair. Someone else experiences sorrow and uses it as an opportunity to better love God and other people.

9. See John 11:35.
10. See Revelation 21:1–27.

Think of Judas. He sinned and felt remorse. He then committed suicide. Consider Peter. He too sinned and felt remorse. Unlike Judas, he used those feeling to lead him to repentance and back to Jesus.

Let sorrow lead us to charity and compassion. When we experience grief and sadness, let us use it as an opportunity to identify with the heart of God.

WHAT IF I AM NOT EXPERIENCING CHRISTIAN JOY?

There can be several reasons why we may not be experiencing the virtue of joy, and all are rooted in that fact that nearness to God brings joy, while distance from God brings sadness.

The prime reason for distance from God is sin. That is why John the Baptist preached repentance, conversion, and the spiritual washing of baptism. Reflect again on the Canticle of Zechariah.

> And [John's] father Zechari'ah was filled with the
> Holy Spirit, and prophesied, saying, . . .
> "You, child, will be called the prophet of the Most
> High; for you will go before the Lord to prepare
> his ways, to give knowledge of salvation to his
> people in the forgiveness of their sins,
> through the tender mercy of our God,
> when the day shall dawn upon us from on high
> to give light to those who sit in darkness and in
> the shadow of death, to guide our feet into the
> way of peace." (Luke 1:67, 76–79)

That peace of which Zechariah speaks is peace with God and it comes through forgiveness of sin. St. John the Baptist told everyone and anyone who would listen that if they wanted peace, they must grow close to God. If they wanted to grow close to God, they must repent of their sins. All sin robs us of joy because sin distances us from Christ, the source of joy. However, some sins especially affect a person's joy. By way of example, I'll point out four of what are called capital or deadly sins.

The *greedy* person knows no joy. His desire to accumulate things is never satisfied. *Envy* stirs up within the person a continuing dissatisfaction with what he has in comparison with that of other people. *Lust*, a third capital sin, can give the illusion of satisfaction but it is always brief and it makes the sinner a slave to sensual passions. There is no joy in a prison made by sin. Then there is *pride*, a sin that requires a lot of work. The prideful person struggles to make sure others see him as a success. That often means making others look bad in comparison to himself. The prideful person loses the joy of true friendship because he cannot treat another as an equal.

If we seek the joy of Christmas, we must walk up to the crèche in our parish church unencumbered by sin. Conversion is the way to joy and it is the message that John the Baptist speaks to us through the readings at Mass during Advent.

PRAY LESS, JOYLESS

A second obstacle to joy is a failure to pray. Again, it is about closeness to Jesus. We can ask ourselves "Do I pray at all?" or "Is my prayer an encounter with the living God or is it just some words thrown at the wall?" If I don't find joy as a virtue in my life, I need to examine my conscience about my prayer life.

Prayer should be a real encounter with God. Read the Psalms and see how often the psalmist starts his prayer with an emotion, perhaps anger or sadness, and see how the psalmist ends his prayer. Let me give you one example. Jesus quoted Psalm 22 from the Cross. The author begins with an anguished cry to God.

> ² My God, my God, why have you abandoned me?
> Why so far from my call for help,
> from my cries of anguish?
> ³ My God, I call by day, but you do not answer;
> by night, but I have no relief. ...

⁷ But I am a worm, not a man,
  scorned by men, despised by the people.
⁸ All who see me mock me;
  they curl their lips and jeer;
  they shake their heads at me:
⁹ "He relied on the LORD—let him deliver him;
  if he loves him, let him rescue him." (NAB)

These are not the words of a happy man, but they *are* the words of a prayerful man—someone taking his problems to the Lord. Listen to how the complaint of the psalmist turns to petition:

²⁰ LORD, do not stay far off;
  my strength, come quickly to help me.
²¹ Deliver my soul from the sword,
  my life from the grip of the dog.
²² Save me from the lion's mouth,
  my poor life from the horns of wild bulls. (NAB)

The psalmist then turns to praise.

²³ Then I will proclaim your name to my brethren;
  in the assembly I will praise you:
²⁴ "You who fear the LORD, give praise!
  All descendants of Jacob, give honor;
  show reverence, all descendants of Israel!
²⁵ For he has not spurned or disdained
  the misery of this poor wretch,
  Did not turn away from me,
  but heard me when I cried out.
²⁶ I will offer praise in the great assembly;
  my vows I will fulfill before those who fear him.
²⁷ The poor will eat their fill;
  those who seek the LORD will offer praise. ...

²⁸ All the ends of the earth
    will remember and turn to the LORD;
    All the families of nations
    will bow low before him.
²⁹ For kingship belongs to the LORD,
    the ruler over the nations. (NAB)

In the thirty-two verses of this psalm, the author moves from sadness, anger, complaint to petition and finally to praise of God for His power and goodness. That is a model of prayer. We must honestly lay our lives before the Lord in prayer. We must seek his help and entrust our concerns and ourselves to Him—placing everything in His hands. Then we thank and praise Him for His goodness and mercy. Like the father, who in seeking healing for his son, said to Jesus, "Lord, I believe, help my unbelief" (Mark 9:22–24), we can say, "Lord I rejoice in You, help my lack of joy," or hope, or peace, or whatever virtue we want or need. When we encounter God in prayer, He can strengthen us in joy, hope, trust, acceptance, and perspective.

UNDERSTAND GOD'S PLAN

The third hindrance to closeness to God and the joy accompanying it is a lack of understanding of the kingdom John the Baptist proclaimed and Jesus brought into existence. The world has a non-Christian perspective. There was a time when society upheld some Christian morality, but it does so only minimally now. Therefore, it is vitally important that we immerse ourselves in God's Word. To understand the kingdom there is no better tool than the Bible. If you are not regularly reading Scripture, make it a habitual part of your life. You could start with the Sunday readings, prayerfully meditating on them during the week. Read the daily Mass readings. Many programs will help you read key sections of Scripture in an organized way over time. There are also books on the life of Christ that tell the story of Jesus in an orderly fashion. While not Scripture, in combination with Scripture they can be helpful.[11] Also, read good Catholic literature.[12] We are also blessed to have Catholic radio and television, and study programs available on the Web.

Self-Reliance versus Spirit-Reliance

The final hindrance is lack of reliance on the Holy Spirit. When I am the guide for my life, I'm in trouble. However, if God the Holy Spirit is my guide, I have a life with direction, joy, and meaning. How to discern what is from the Holy Spirit is a topic too broad to explore in this book.[13] However, it is important to note that we need to seek God's guidance and prudently discern His will. In doing so, we will experience His protection.

> Seek the Lord your God, and you will find him, if you search after him with all your heart and with all your soul. When you are in tribulation, and all these things come upon you in the latter days, you will return to the Lord your God and obey his voice, for the Lord your God is a merciful God; he will not fail you or destroy you or forget the covenant with your fathers which he swore to them. (Deuteronomy 4:29–31)

How to Grow in the Virtue of Joy

The pop psychology of positive thinking and self-talk is pretty useless. I could tell myself a thousand times each and every day

---

11. For example, Frank Sheed, *To Know Christ Jesus*; Bishop Fulton J. Sheen, *The Life of Christ*; Archbishop Alban Goodier, *The Public Life of Jesus Christ*; Giuseppe Ricciotti, *The Life of Christ*; and Henri Daniel-Rops, *Jesus and His Times*.

12. Make sure that you choose a publisher that prints books reflecting the mind of the Church. Orthodoxy is important. As of May 2014, there is a good reference list at http://www.aquinasandmore.com/catholic-articles/how-to-choose-catholic-books-and-publishers/article/90/sort/relevance/productsperpage/12/layout/grid/currentpage/1. My favorite publishers are Emmaus Road Publishing, Ignatius Press, Our Sunday Visitor, Scepter Publishers, Sophia Institute Press, and Word Among Us Press.

13. Father Timothy M. Gallagher has written widely on this topic. I suggest *Discerning the Will of God: An Ignatian Guide to Christian Decision Making* (Chestnut Ridge, NY: The Crossroad Publishing Company, 2009). As of May 2014 audio of Father Gallagher is available for free at www.discerninghearts.org.

that I have a wonderful singing voice. However, every time I try to utter a note or sing a chorus, the truth will become apparent. I don't have any ability as a singer.

But there is a type of self-talk that can be helpful. We can call it truth-talk. I hope that we are already using it. Haven't we all, when confronted with a temptation, heard a little voice saying, "You can't resist this temptation" or "go ahead; it's not that big of a sin." We should counter that voice by reminding ourselves of the truth. God gives me the grace to overcome this temptation. He only speaks the truth and I can rely on Him. We can also ask the saints to help us, in particular, by saying a "Hail Mary," asking our Lady's assistance.

Sometimes self-evangelization is helpful. When we evangelize others, we tell them the "Good News" of the Gospel. At times, we need to hear the "Good News" again—to re-evangelize ourselves. Some of our Protestant brethren encourage their congregations to memorize Scriptures for this very purpose. We can do the same.

John the Baptist relied on the Scriptures. When the priests and the Levites asked John who he was, John responded by quoting from Isaiah 40: "I am the voice of one crying in the wilderness, 'Make straight the way of the Lord'" (John 1:23). What did that do for John? It put his life and message in perspective. He was saying, don't try to make me more than I am. He's telling the priests and the Levites that he is not the Messiah. He is also affirming who he is in God. He has a mission and he is fulfilling that vocation.

Joy is built into the knowledge and acceptance of who I am and am not. To know who I am in God is freeing. So, if I fall and sin, the world doesn't end. I get up, dust myself off, ask God's forgiveness, ask for His help so I don't fall again, and then I get back on the trail of what God wants me to do. That's freeing; that gives right perspective; that situates us in joy. That perspective keeps pride at bay.

Speaking the truth to myself also keeps me from the sadness that spiritual writers tell us is from the devil. You probably have heard it from time to time. That little voice that says, "You're no good. God can't love you. Your work serves no purpose." John guarded against that trap by saying exactly who he was in God— He was the voice in the desert. John knew his calling; he knew his vocation. Moreover, he wasn't afraid to tell it to his detractors and, in so doing, remind himself that he was doing what God called him to do.

Here is an example. Parenting in the twenty-first century can be quite a challenge. Many feel inadequate to the task. When those feelings creep into your thoughts, you need to do exactly what John the Baptist did. Speak the truth. First, affirm that God is giving you the grace to be a father or mother to your children. Sure, it will be a struggle. There will be pain; there will be sorrow, but God will be with you. Do not despair!

Remember When

Another exercise can help you. Memorialize your "testimony." Ask God to help you see where He has worked in your life.[14] Write it down and use it as a tool in self-evangelization, recalling what God has done for you in the past.

The Passover celebration did that for the Jewish people, and at every Passover they recall that God saved them from the bondage in Egypt and brought them to the Promised Land. That is their corporate testimony. Their present situation may be wonderful and rosy or it may be difficult and disappointing, but by recalling the Passover and celebrating it they were saying, "God cared for us in the past; we trust Him to care for us in the present."

Try doing that on a personal level. I recommend you take pen in hand and prayerfully write out what God has already done in your life and how he has brought you to where you are today, i.e. write out your testimony. It's a freeing and joy-giving exercise.

14. See my book *God's on the Phone: Stories of Grace in Action* (Cincinnati, OH: Servant Book 2011).

AN ETERNAL PERSPECTIVE

Also, what I call an "eternal perspective" is very helpful. If we have an understanding of God's long-term plan for us as individuals and for creation as a whole, we will be able to make sense of our life today and order it in such a way to attain life in the kingdom of God.[15] Even though God's kingdom will not be fully realized until the Second Coming of Christ, we can still feel the effects of the victory of Jesus in our lives today.

Let me use the example of a man in a dense forest who wants to get to the base of a mountain. If that man only looks at what is around him, he is going to get lost. However, if he looks up at the mountain, it will guide his steps.

It's the same with us. If we only look at the circumstances around us, we can lose perspective. All of us go through difficult circumstances, trials, and tribulations. It is then that we need most to consider the promises of God. He is always true to His word and is totally trustworthy. I might be stuck in the mud right now but if I look to God, I have a hope that is sure because it is based upon God's promises. With that perspective I find a peace and, indeed, the joy that accompanies it. The infant John the Baptist would encourage us to do so.

Let me end this chapter with words from Pope Francis, a person whose joy in the Lord is obvious.

> There are Christians whose lives seem like Lent without Easter. I realize of course that joy is not expressed the same way at all times in life, especially at moments of great difficulty. Joy adapts and changes, but it always endures, even as a flicker of light born of our personal certainty that, when everything is said and done, we are infinitely loved. I understand the grief of people who have to endure

---

15. For a fuller treatment of this theme, see Regis J. Flaherty, *Last Things First*.

great suffering, yet slowly but surely we all have to let the joy of faith slowly revive as a quiet yet firm trust, even amid the greatest distress: "My soul is bereft of peace; I have forgotten what happiness is. . . . But this I call to mind, and therefore I have hope: the steadfast love of the Lord never ceases, his mercies never come to an end; they are new every morning. Great is your faithfulness. . . . It is good that one should wait quietly for the salvation of the Lord" (Lamentations 3:17, 21–23, 26).[16]

FOR PERSONAL REFLECTION AND APPLICATION

- Take my recommendation. Prayerfully write some of the history of your relationship with God. Keep it in your Bible. When you read in Scripture the stories of God working with His people, remember that your story belongs there too.
- Does suffering and sorrow have value in your life? Read the following Scriptures and reflect on their meaning in your circumstances. 1 Peter 4:12–13; Psalms 119:67; Romans 5:3–4.

---

16. Pope Francis, *Evangelii Gaudium*, I.6.

John the Baptist
Man on a Mission

Have you seen any of the Catholic tee-shirts? I own a couple. Messages are emblazoned on front and back, phrases including "totally Catholic" and "pro-life." One even contains the text of the Apostles' Creed!

When I first saw them at a Catholic conference, I bought matching shirts for my youngest daughter and me. I thought it would be wonderful for us to wear them on the same day—sort of a team witness effort. On our first outing, a trip to a supermarket, we drew considerable attention from fellow shoppers. My daughter was oblivious to the interest we were generating. I, however, became very self-conscious. Reactions varied widely. Some smiled; a few scowled; and others had looks of bewilderment.

When we were checking out, the cashier said, "I like your shirts." Then after a quick glance to the right and left she whispered, "I'm Catholic, too!" As we headed to the car, an older man ran to catch up with us. "I'm not a Catholic, but I just wanted you to know that I respect someone who's not afraid to proclaim his faith." As we loaded the groceries into the car, a teenager gave me a thumbs-up after reading the shirt, saying, "keep on, brother!"

Despite the encouragement, I felt *very* uncomfortable. I was glad to get home and out of public view.

I'm not sure if John the Baptist experienced any embarrassment. He certainly stood out in a crowd. The Jews couldn't ignore him. He had a passionate personality. When someone met him and heard his message, they either loved or hated him. He was not a man with shades of grey.

Consider what Mark tells us in the first chapter of his Gospel. "John [the] Baptist appeared in the desert. . . . [He] was clothed in camel's hair, with a leather belt around his waist" (v. 4). Then consider his unusual diet. "He fed on locusts and wild honey" (v. 6). I'm sure that raised some eyebrows.

He also didn't present a particularly popular message. "John the Baptist appeared . . . proclaiming a baptism of repentance for the forgiveness of sins" (Mark 1:4). Repentance is seldom popular.

Yet, despite John's odd behavior and unpopular message, Mark the Evangelist tells us, "People of the whole Judean countryside and all the inhabitants of Jerusalem were going out to him and were being baptized by him in the Jordan River as they acknowledged their sins" (Mark 1:5, NAB). John and his message affected people and changed lives. Many viewed him as a prophet, someone who was proclaiming and applying God's plan for that particular time in history.

ON A MISSION

John had focus. He embraced his vocation and trusted in God's guidance. He had an unshakable self-identity and an understanding of his mission. People identified him with the great prophet Elijah, and with good reason. Elijah lived in the Northern Kingdom of Israel in the ninth century BC, and the Israelites had fallen into worshiping false gods. Even King Ahab and his wife Jezebel led people away from Yahweh into idolatry. Elijah, whose name means, "My God is Yahweh," was outspoken in his condemnation of idolatry and his defense of the Covenant that God made and renewed with Israel throughout her history.

One story is enough to give you insight into Elijah's ministry, spirit, and approach. In 1 Kings 18, Elijah speaks to King Ahab:

"Now therefore send and gather all Israel to me at Mount Carmel, and the four hundred and fifty prophets of Ba´al and the four hundred prophets of Ashe´rah, who eat at Jez´ebel's table."

So Ahab sent to all the people of Israel, and gathered the prophets together at Mount Carmel. And Eli´jah came near to all the people, and said, "How long will you go limping with two different opinions? If the Lord is God, follow him; but if Ba´al, then follow him." . . . Eli´jah said to the people, "I, even I only, am left a prophet of the Lord; but Ba´al's prophets are four hundred and fifty men. Let two bulls be given to us; and let them choose one bull for themselves, and cut it in pieces and lay it on the wood, but put no fire to it; and I will prepare the other bull and lay it on the wood, and put no fire to it. And you call on the name of your god and I will call on the name of the Lord; and the God who answers by fire, he is God." And all the people answered, "It is well spoken." . . . The prophets of Ba´al . . . took the bull which was given them, and they prepared it, and called on the name of Ba´al from morning until noon, saying, "O Ba´al, answer us!" But there was no voice, and no one answered. And they limped about the altar which they had made. And at noon Eli´jah mocked them, saying, "Cry aloud, for he is a god; either he is musing, or he has gone aside, or he is on a journey, or perhaps he is asleep and must be awakened." And they cried aloud, and cut themselves after their custom with swords and lances, until the blood gushed out upon them. And as midday passed, they raved on until the time of the offering of the oblation, but there was no voice; no one answered, no one heeded.

Then Eli'jah said to all the people, "Come near to me"; and . . . he repaired the altar of the Lord that had been thrown down; Eli'jah took twelve stones . . . and with the stones he built an altar in the name of the Lord. And he made a trench about the altar, as great as would contain two measures of seed. And he put the wood in order, and cut the bull in pieces and laid it on the wood. And he said, "Fill four jars with water, and pour it on the burnt offering, and on the wood." And he said, "Do it a second time"; and they did it a second time. And he said, "Do it a third time"; and they did it a third time. And the water ran round about the altar, and filled the trench also with water.

And at the time of the offering of the oblation, Eli'jah the prophet came near and said, "O Lord, God of Abraham, Isaac, and Israel, let it be known this day that you are God in Israel, and that I am your servant, and that I have done all these things at your word. Answer me, O Lord, answer me, that this people may know that you, O Lord, are God, and that you have turned their hearts back." Then the fire of the Lord fell, and consumed the burnt offering, and the wood, and the stones, and the dust, and licked up the water that was in the trench. And when all the people saw it, they fell on their faces; and they said, "The Lord, he is God; the Lord, he is God." (1 Kings 18:19–39)

When I read that passage, I can't help seeing, in my mind's eye, Elijah sitting in a lounge chair, under an umbrella, sipping lemonade while the priests of Baal try to get a fire started! Elijah wasn't cocky but he was sure. He knew the true God. He knew that he was the Lord's prophet. He knew he had a message to deliver. And he trusted God. We see the same personality in John the Baptist. A man on God's mission, obedient and trusting the Lord.

What became of Elijah? Scripture tells us that at the end of his earthly life, Elijah was taken up into heaven in a flaming chariot drawn by fiery horses in the midst of a whirlwind.[1] It was thereafter believed that Elijah would return when the arrival of the promised Messiah was near.

The sight of John preaching at the Jordan, wearing the type of clothing that Elijah had worn,[2] caused many people to wonder. In fact, Jesus said,

> Truly, I say to you, among those born of women there has risen no one greater than John the Baptist; yet he who is least in the kingdom of heaven is greater than he. From the days of John the Baptist until now the kingdom of heaven has suffered violence, and men of violence take it by force. For all the prophets and the law prophesied until John; and if you are willing to accept it, he is Eli'jah who is to come. (Matthew 11:11–14)

Although not literally Elijah,[3] John the Baptist fulfilled the same office and ministry as Elijah. He called the Jews back to the one true God. Like Elijah, John was fearless because he trusted God.

What was the fate of John the Baptist, precursor of Christ and proclaimer of the message of God? Quite literally he lost his head by order of Herod.[4] He was a martyr.

---

1. See 2 Kings 2:1–12.
2. See 2 Kings 1:8.
3. See John 1:21.
4. See Matthew 14:1–12 and Mark 6:14–29.

Christian Prophets Who Paid the Price

The prophetic ministry didn't end with Elijah. It didn't end with John the Baptist. Throughout the history of the Church, from Pentecost until today, we find men and women who continue the ministry of Elijah and John the Baptist. One such person was Blessed Franz Jägerstätter (1907–1943).[5] This is a man that could be any of us. He was a layman, a husband, a father, *and* a martyr. Born in 1907 in Austria, Franz did not particularly stand out from his neighbors. That is until the rise of Nazism in the 1930s. While most people in Austria were embracing Nazism, Franz became more rooted in his Catholic faith. He examined the philosophy of Hitler and the truths of the Catholic faith, and he was convinced that they were incompatible.

While many citizens knelt in the streets when the Nazi army entered Austria, Franz would only bow to God. Yet, he wasn't a part of the resistance and he wasn't a revolutionary, but he did point out the incompatibility between Nazism and Christianity. Like St. Thomas More, he upheld the truth without directly confronting the government. Eventually Franz was forced to take a stand when he was drafted in 1943. He said that he would not fight but was willing to do non-violent service, such as working in the medical corps. His request was denied, but Franz held firm. The Nazis arrested, tried, and condemned him to death for sedition.

Some tried to induce him to give into the Nazis. They pointed out that as a husband and father his family needed him. Jägerstätter stated, "I cannot believe that, just because one has a wife and children, a man is free to offend God." His jailers were amazed at his peace. As his death approached he wrote, "If I must write . . . with my hands in chains, I find that much better than if my will were in chains. Neither prison nor chains nor sentence of death can rob a man of the faith and his free will. God gives so much strength that it is possible to bear any suffering."[6]

---

5. For a fuller biography as of June 2014, see http://www.vatican.va/news_services/liturgy/saints/ns_lit_doc_20071026_jagerstatter_en.html.

6. "Bl. Franz Jägerstätter (1907–1943)" as of June 2014 available at http://www.vatican.va/news_services/liturgy/saints/ns_lit_doc_20071026_jagerstatter_en.html.

The role of prophet and proclaimer of God's Word is not limited to males. A Catholic laywoman, who certainly lived the life of a prophet, was the Servant of God Dorothy Day.[7] She not only championed the poor, she embraced personal poverty. She fought for the dignity of workers and for civil rights. Like those who met John the Baptist, people had strong feelings about her. Just as John was both hated and loved, Dorothy Day angered some in Church hierarchy and inspired others. But she always strove to live and proclaim the Gospel.

AND US

Prophets like Elijah and John the Baptist are calling out to us right now. Catholics, like Blessed Franz Jägerstätter and the Servant of God Dorothy Day, are also calling you and me. The Right Rev. Ottokar Prohaszka, author of *Meditations on the Gospels*, wrote, "Precursors [like John the Baptist] are necessary at all times."

History boasts a long line of men and women who embraced the mission God gave them, and suffered the consequences at the hands of a world that would not accept their prophetic witness. Today each of us is to follow that holy path. We need to identify our mission and live it within our sphere of influence and in a manner consistent with our vocation (wife, husband, single person, ordained, or consecrated religious). As we live that mission, we will be witnesses, precursors, men and women pointing to Jesus.

So how do we become God-fearing radicals like John the Baptist? Live the Beatitudes!

> Blessed are the poor in spirit, for theirs is the kingdom of heaven.
> Blessed are those who mourn, for they shall be comforted.
> Blessed are the meek, for they shall inherit the earth.
> Blessed are those who hunger and thirst for righteousness, for they shall be satisfied.

---

7. See her biography by Jim Forest, available as of June 2014 at http://www.catholicworker.org/dorothyday/ddbiographytext.cfm?Number=72.

Blessed are the merciful, for they shall obtain mercy.

Blessed are the pure in heart, for they shall see God.

Blessed are the peacemakers, for they shall be called sons of God.

Blessed are those who are persecuted for righteousness' sake, for theirs is the kingdom of heaven.

Blessed are you when men revile you and persecute you and utter all kinds of evil against you falsely on my account. Rejoice and be glad, for your reward is great in heaven, for so men persecuted the prophets who were before you.

(Matthew 5:3–12)

I'll focus on three Beatitudes that I believe are particularly needed in Western culture: poverty of spirit, hunger and thirst for righteousness, and willingness to suffer persecution.

POVERTY OF SPIRIT

John was an ascetic who espoused material and spiritual poverty. We too are called to choose a sober lifestyle in imitation not only of John the Baptist but of the One to whom John pointed. St. Paul, quite a prophet in his own right, wrote that Jesus "though he was rich, yet for your sake he became poor, so that by his poverty you might become rich" (2 Corinthians 8:9).

John the Baptist's poverty entailed more than merely not owning things. It required placing God's will above his own and insuring that the message was about God and not about self. John wasn't concerned about self-satisfaction, self-absorption, self-seeking, self-sufficiency, self-centeredness, self-interest, self-preservation, or self-will. John was about serving God, being God's man, following God's plan and not his own. John lived spiritual poverty. God calls us to the same standard.

Consider what the Catechism teaches about poverty of spirit.

Jesus enjoins his disciples to prefer him to every-thing and everyone, and bids them "renounce all that [they have]" for his sake and that of the Gos-pel.[8] Shortly before his passion he gave them the example of the poor widow of Jerusalem who, out of her poverty, gave all that she had to live on.[9] The precept of detachment from riches is obligatory for entrance into the Kingdom of heaven. (2544)

According to the Glossary to the *Catechism of the Catholic Church*, "Poverty of spirit signifies detachment from worldly things and voluntary humility."

In praying the Our Father we are asking for poverty of spirit as we say, "Thy Kingdom come, thy will be done." These words echo Jesus' prayer to His (and our) Father from the Garden of Gethsemane, "Not my will, but yours, be done!" (Luke 22:42).

The poor in spirit can say with St. Paul,

Whatever gain I had, I counted as loss for the sake of Christ. Indeed I count everything as loss because of the surpassing worth of knowing Christ Jesus my Lord. For his sake I have suffered the loss of all things, and count them as refuse, in order that I may gain Christ and be found in him. (Philippians 3:7–9)

This norm should have very practical application in our lives. One way to foster poverty of spirit is to tithe. Tithing is a tan-gible expression of our dependence on God. After all, our time, talent, and treasure are gifts from God. We are stewards, not own-ers. Examine your heart in light of this Scripture passage from Matthew: "Where your treasure is, there will your heart be also" (6:21). Ask yourself, "What would I be unwilling to give up if

8. Lk 14:33; cf. Mk 8:35.
9. Cf. Lk 21:4.

asked to do so? What are the things that I feel I can't do without?" Our answer will show us how detached we really are.

The poor of spirit are truly free to be about God's agenda, as was St. John the Baptist. Their trust is in God, not in riches of this world. If we are clinging to certain material possessions, our hands are full and unable to receive the good gifts, which God wants to give us. Moreover, generosity is a virtue that accompanies poverty of spirit and disposes us to value others more than our possessions.

In addition, poverty of spirit incorporates non-tangible riches. Here ask, "How do I react when someone challenges me? How much do I want recognition? Do I have to have my own way in certain areas? Do I get upset when 'my time' is interrupted?" Humility and detachment always accompany poverty of spirit.

HUNGER AND THIRST FOR RIGHTEOUSNESS

Hunger and thirst point to very basic needs. If we do not have food and drink, we can't sustain physical life. We not only can't help others, we die. Without righteousness we can't sustain a healthy spiritual life and we can't reach out to others. The essence of righteousness is conformity to God's will—the *right* relationship with Him

Jesus personally shows us how to be righteous. He tells us that He only does that which His Father directs Him to do.[10] Jesus said, "I have not spoken on my own authority; the Father who sent me has himself given me commandment what to say and what to speak" (John 12:49).

To follow the example of John the Baptist, we must seek God's will and do it. We need a heart and a mind ready to obey.

PREPARE FOR PERSECUTION AND MARTYRDOM

"Blessed are those who are persecuted for righteousness' sake" (Matthew 5:10). In many countries in the world, Christians are

---

10. See John 5:19.

being persecuted and killed at an alarming rate. Pope Francis stated, "Nowadays, persecution of Christians is stronger than it was in the first centuries of the Church, and there are more Christian martyrs than in that time."[11]

We in the United States only catch a glimpse of that persecution when the media occasionally reports on it. However, our own society is becoming more secular and anti-Christian. Increasingly, it is politically incorrect to express one's Christian faith in the public arena.

Considering how often our society is at variance with Christian truth, I would venture to suggest that if we are not experiencing some pushback, we aren't living as prophets and as Christ's disciples.

John the Baptist was a martyr for the faith. If we are to assume his role, we also must be ready for martyrdom. Bishop Fulton Sheen talked about two types of martyrs: red martyrs and white martyrs. Red martyrs are those who actually shed their blood for Christ. Think of those who have died for the faith starting with St. Stephen up to those martyred today in countries in the Middle East, in parts of India, and other places around the world.

White martyrs suffer for the faith but are not actually killed. Call to mind those imprisoned in China and Vietnam, and those who have to live as second-class citizens in many strict Muslim countries, such as Saudi Arabia. Think about those who suffer in our own culture. The pharmacist who refuses to dispense abortifacient drugs or the teacher who tries to bring God into the discussion in a public school. Think of the person who works for an unethical employer and refuses to overbill for a service, thus putting their job in jeopardy. Below is one of my favorite poems. It speaks of the cost of true disciples.

---

11. Pope Francis speaking on the first day of a two-day international congress in Rome, entitled "Religious Freedom According to International Law and Global Conflict of Values," and delivered on June 20, 2014. Available as of June 2014 at http://www.zenit.org/en/articles/pope-unprecedented-religious-persecution-can-t-go-on.

NO SCAR?

"For to you it has been granted on behalf of
Christ, not only to believe in Him, but also to
suffer for His sake."
Philippians 1:29

Hast thou no scar?
No hidden scar on foot, or side, or hand?
I hear thee sung as mighty in the land;
I hear them hail thy bright, ascendant star.
Hast thou no scar?

Hast thou no wound?
Yet I was wounded by the archers; spent,
Leaned Me against a tree to die; and rent
By ravening beasts that compassed Me, I swooned.
Hast thou no wound?

No wound? No scar?
Yet, as the Master shall the servant be,
And pierced are the feet that follow Me.
But thine are whole; can he have followed far
Who hast no wound or scar?[12]

If we live the Christian life, we should expect to experience
trials. And we need to be prepared.

Living in the desert, and fasting by only eating locusts and
wild honey were part of John's preparation for martyrdom. The
desert experience points to prayer, and John's diet points to fasting. Indeed, prayer and fasting are indispensable parts of the life
of every Catholic.

The Church encourages Catholics to practice mortification,
saying no to self as a means to saying a full-hearted yes to God.

---

12. Poem by Amy Carmichael cited in Elisabeth Elliot, *A Chance to Die: The Life and Leg-
acy of Amy Carmichael* (Old Tappan, NJ: Fleming H. Revell Company, 1987), 264.

This focus is also part of our preparation for martyrdom—whether red or white.

To a Tee

Let me end by going back to my story about the tee-shirts with the Catholic themes. Over time, I grew more comfortable with the shirts. The positive, reinforcing comments outnumber the dirty looks. I've also engaged in some discussions because of the messages on the apparel, especially about prolife issues.

The approach may not be for everyone, but the concept is worth considering. We shouldn't be ashamed to let people know we're Christian. St. Paul was not reluctant. In his letter to the Romans, he tells us, "I am not ashamed of the gospel" (Romans 1:16).

Some people use bumper stickers. Some wear a small cross on their lapel or blouse. For me displaying some visible sign of my faith helps me to better live it. If I put a Christian message on the car bumper, I realize that I need to repent of any bad driving habits and make a change, lest I bring shame upon that Gospel message.

Now, a bumper sticker or a message on a shirt shouldn't determine how I act. Love for God and for His people should motivate me. However, I will take any help I can get! The tangible sign makes me a little more accountable for my actions. Being more accountable makes me a better witness.

The key to the process is to be sure that the tee-shirt, sticker, or lapel cross reflect the life and faith I *live*. These externals are not witnesses in and of themselves; however, when tied to a Christian life, there is a prophetic witness—not unlike that of John the Baptist—and an opportunity to have an impact for Christ.

One final thought: If it was illegal to be a Catholic follower of Jesus, would there be enough evidence to convict you? There was enough evidence to convict John the Baptist, Franz Jägerstätter, and many others. May it be so for us.

For Personal Reflection and Application

- Read the lives of some of the canonized saints. Reflect on how they fulfilled God's call in their lives. A good place to start is at the Vatican website, which provides short biographies of recently canonized saints. As of June 2014 see http://www.vatican.va/news_services/liturgy/saints/index_saints_en.html. Be inspired by their example and ask for their intercession and help.

- Read again the Beatitudes as listed above. Consider the radical call God gives us through them. What Beatitude is God calling you to embrace right now in your life?

JOHN THE BAPTIST
Pointing to Jesus[1]
Overcoming Obstacles to Conversion
❦

Our recent popes have called us to a new evangelization. John the Baptist was ahead of his time. He was responding to that call two thousand years ago.

Calling lapsed Catholics back to active participation in the faith is a major element of the new evangelization. In the time of Jesus, many Jews, like many Catholics today, had wandered from God's call and His plan for them as the chosen people. For example, the Sadducees[2] were more concerned about maintaining their power than in responding to God. They were cynics.

On the other hand, the scribes and Pharisees[3] appeared religious, but it was often a distorted and legalistic version of the

---

1. The outline for this chapter is taken primarily from a sermon by St. Francis de Sales for the Fourth Sunday of Advent found in *The Sermons of St. Francis de Sales for Advent and Christmas*, vol. 4 in the series, trans. Nuns of the Visitation, ed. Father Lewis S. Fiorelli, O.S.F.S. (Rockford, IL: Tan Books and Publishers, Inc., 1987). Hereafter referred to as *Sermons* in the footnotes.

2. "Known for their denial of the bodily resurrection, the Sadducees came from the leading families of the nation—the priests, merchants, and aristocrats. The high priests and the most powerful members of the priesthood were mainly Sadducees (Acts 5:17)." Herbert Lockyer, Sr., General Editor, *Nelson's Bible Dictionary* (Nashville, TN: Thomas Nelson Publishers, 1986), 936.

3. "A religious and political party, . . . the Pharisees were known for insisting that the law of God be observed as the scribes interpreted it. . . . The Pharisees thought they could match God's standards by keeping all the outward rules." Lockyer, *Nelson's Bible Dictionary*, 830.

faith of Israel. They were concerned with the letter of the law—not only the commandments found in Scripture but the many other regulations that had developed over the years. There were certainly well intentioned scribes and Pharisees. However, too often, their rigorous religious life led them to pride. Still others were merely hypocrites. Jesus said of them, "They bind heavy burdens, hard to bear, and lay them on men's shoulders; but they themselves will not move them with their finger. They do all their deeds to be seen by men" (Matthew 23:4–5).

In two previous chapters we looked at John's message of joy. However, the primary message that the adult John delivered during his public ministry was one of repentance and conversion. He was an evangelist calling his fellow Jews back to the essence of the Jewish faith and pointing them to the approaching fulfillment of the Old Covenant.

PENITENCE

In this John had a one-track mind—a very healthy one-track mind. He kept pointing to the imminent arrival of the Messiah and the need for personal repentance as the key preparation. In John, the man was the message and the message formed the man. His lifestyle, actions, and words centered on the dual aspects of his proclamation—repent and prepare.

Some people wanted to make John the focal point, but he unfailingly turns the attention to Jesus.[4] Priests, Levites,[5] and Pharisees question him about his identity and mission. He answers their questions as briefly as possible, so that attention is not given to him but to the Messiah.

> The Jews sent priests and Levites from Jerusalem
> to ask him, "Who are you?" [John] confessed,
> he did not deny, but confessed, "I am not the

---

4. See John 1:15–37.

5. Levites were "descendants of Levi who served as assistants to the Priests in the worship system of the nation of Israel." Lockyer, *Nelson's Bible Dictionary*, 644.

Christ." And they asked him, "What then? Are you Elijah?" He said, "I am not." "Are you the prophet?" And he answered, "No." They said to him then, "Who are you? Let us have an answer for those who sent us. What do you say about yourself?" He said, "I am the voice of one crying in the wilderness, 'Make straight the way of the Lord,' as the prophet Isaiah said." (John 1:19–23)

Later, as recorded in John the Evangelist's Gospel, the Baptist "saw Jesus coming toward him, and said, 'Behold, the Lamb of God, who takes away the sin of the world! This is he of whom I said, "After me comes a man who ranks before me, for he was before me"'" (John 1:29–30).

John didn't want to discuss himself. John wanted the attention on "the one who is coming after me, whose sandal strap I am not worthy to untie" (John 1:27). It's a good lesson for us. Is life "all about me" or am I pointing to God and His kingdom in what I do and say?

Act Now

There was urgency to the Baptist's message of repentance. He preaches at the banks of the Jordan River. He says repent *now*, not tomorrow. He invites those who hear his preaching to step into the water of the Jordan and be baptized without delay.

Apparently, John baptized many people, but there were those who turned away because they "rejected the purpose of God for *themselves*" (Luke 7:30, emphasis added).

It is the same today. Some people don't benefit from the preaching of the Gospel because, even though they hear the message, they don't act on it.

Procrastination

One reason for lack of response is procrastination. No one is guaranteed a tomorrow, so there should be a sense of urgency to respond to the Gospel. St. Josemaria Escriva writes, "Why don't you give yourself to God once and for all . . . , truly . . . , now?"[6] He also states, "Don't wait until the New Year to make your resolutions. Every day is a good day to make good decisions. *Hodie, nunc!*—Today, now!"[7]

Failure to repent can have eternal consequences. The best prevention against an untimely death—dying in state of sin—is to live each day as your last. Delay is always a bad choice.

In high school, a nun told my wife's religion class, "When God calls, respond. You never know when or if He will call again. You don't want to miss the opportunity." Shortly after hearing those words, my wife was babysitting for a couple while they were at a prayer meeting. While driving my wife home, the father of the family engaged her in conversation. At one point he told her, "I think the Lord is calling you right now." Immediately my wife recalled what the nun had told her. She accepted the call there and then, and her life and relationship with God changed from that day onward.

God's call demands a timely and determined response. I am reminded of Luke 19:51 that describes Jesus' attitude in fulfilling His Father's directions. "When the days drew near for him to be received up, he set his face to go to Jerusalem." He was decisive. When His Father called Him to Calvary, He let nothing stand in the way.

St. Francis de Sales said, "How dare we put off doing what we have heard to be useful for our conversion, since our whole life really depends on each present moment when we hear what must be done."[8] This is the message of John the Baptist. It is the message of Advent.

---

6. The Way, 902. As of June 2014 the writings of St. Josemaria Escriva are available online at http://www.escrivaworks.org/.
7. The Forge, 163. As of June 2014 the writings of St. Josemaria Escriva are available online at http://www.escrivaworks.org/.
8. St. Francis de Sales, *Sermons*, 39.

Presumption

Some, who heard the message of the Baptist or who hear the preaching of the Gospel today, don't take action because they only concentrate on the mercy of God to the exclusion of His justice. These people say, "I'm generally a good person, surely God will accept me."

It is never prudent to *presume* on God's mercy. Certainly, God is merciful. In fact, if not for His mercy and forgiveness, no one would be saved. Yet, God is also just—another reason not to delay. St. Francis de Sales states, "Although God is infinitely merciful, He is also infinitely just. When His mercy is . . . presumed, it provokes His justice (cf. Romans 2:4–5)."[9]

Material Avarice

Avarice is one of the capital sins. It is "a passion for riches and their attendant power" (CCC 2552). Inordinate attachment to possessions can get in the way of a timely response to God. We need to remember that material riches will not gain us heaven. No matter how abundant one's material wealth, it eventually rots away.

> [Jesus] told them a parable, saying, "The land of a rich man brought forth plentifully; and he thought to himself, 'What shall I do, for I have nowhere to store my crops?' And he said, 'I will do this: I will pull down my barns, and build larger ones; and there I will store all my grain and my goods. And I will say to my soul, Soul, you have ample goods laid up for many years; take your ease, eat, drink, be merry.' But God said to him, 'Fool! This night your soul is required of you; and the things you have prepared, whose will they be?' So is he who lays up treasure for himself, and is not *rich toward God*." (Luke 12:16–21, emphasis added)

---

9. Ibid., 47.

Recall the directions God gave to the Israelites in the dessert. Daily He sent them manna with the instruction to gather only what they needed for that day.[10] What happened to the manna if they tried to hoard it? It would rot and be inedible.

SPIRITUAL AVARICE

St. Francis de Sales identifies another form of greediness—"spiritual avarice" —that can inhibit embracing God's call. He says that these people seek

> to obtain a great deal of knowledge and to amass a huge stock of devotional exercises. You find some people who never tire of amassing new writings and instructions, all sorts of spiritual advice and information, and who nevertheless do not put any of it into practice! . . . They collect innumerable books and create libraries that are wonders to behold. Poor creatures, what is the purpose in all that?[11]

While material greed is a great disorder, St. John of the Cross intimates that spiritual avarice is potentially much worse. The spiritual version of avarice makes the sinner appear religious, while actually the person is not responding to God. It is the problem Jesus identifies when He says the scribes and the Pharisees are "like whitewashed tombs, which outwardly appear beautiful, but within they are full of dead men's bones and all uncleanness" (Matthew 23:27). It is easy to discern the sin of the person who lusts after material possessions or worldly honors. Those close to him can point out his failing and call him to repentance. However, spiritual avarice is much more subtle. With his nose buried in a spiritual book and with a plethora of religious practices, the man

---

10. The exception was the day prior to the Sabbath when He told them to collect enough for two days.
11. St. Francis de Sales, *Sermons*, 39.

with spiritual avarice appears quite "holy" in many people's eyes. Therefore, people are less likely to challenge him and call him to conversion that he needs.

St. John of the Cross in the *Dark Night of the Soul* writes:

> Many never have enough of listening to counsels and learning spiritual precepts, and of possessing and reading many books. . . . They burden themselves with images and rosaries which are very curious; now they put down one, now take up another; now they change about, now change back again; now they want this kind of thing, now that, preferring one kind of cross to another. . . . Others you will see adorned with [religious medals] and relics and tokens like children with trinkets.[12]

Rather than legitimately using books and sacred objects as means to draw closer to God, the person with spiritual avarice makes them ends in themselves. Again, John of the Cross identifies the root of the problem.

> I condemn the attachment of the heart, and the affection which they have for the nature, multitude and curiosity of these things. . . . True devotion must issue from the heart, and consist in the truth and substance alone of what is represented by spiritual things.[13]

The preaching of John the Baptist sought to pierce through the façade of spiritual avarice, but for many, it was armor they guarded jealously. It kept many from seeking the baptism of re-

---

12. St. John of the Cross, *Dark Night of the Soul*, bk. I, chap. III, no. 1. See Dover Thrift Edition of *Dark Night of the Soul*, trans. E. Allison Peers (Mineola, NY: Dover Publications, 2003), 9.
13. St. John of the Cross, *Dark Night*, 9.

pentance. Unfortunately, this spiritual malady still haunts some Church corridors today. Rosaries, images, devotions are always to be means to draw closer to Christ, and never ends in themselves.

SIN LEADS TO MORE SIN

Hidden, unrepented sin is another reason some people fail to respond to the call of ongoing conversion, whether the call is given by John the Baptist, a priest from the pulpit, or a friend's concern. For example, King David committed adultery with Bathsheba, who then became pregnant. David tried to hide his sin by trickery. He induced Bathsheba's husband Uriah to get drunk in hopes that he would have marital relations with his wife—thereby Uriah and others would assume that Uriah was the father of the unborn child.[14] In doing so, David committed another sin. Next, he successfully arranged to have Uriah killed in battle, another and more grievous sin. Instead of repenting in a timely manner, David tried to hide his sin from man and God—something that is quite impossible.

David eventually did repent, and God forgave, but David had to face the consequences of his sins.[15] The reality is as sure today as it was in Israel when David was king. Concealed and unrepented sin leads to more sins.

MAKING THE ROAD STRAIGHT

Another element of St. John's message harkens to the words of the Prophet Isaiah. Luke quotes Isaiah 40:3–5, "Prepare the way of the Lord, make straight his paths. Every valley shall be filled and every mountain and hill shall be made low. The winding roads shall be made straight" (Luke 3:4–5).

St. Francis de Sales points out that a straight and level road makes travel easier. It's true physically. It's true spiritually. Hills

---

14. Read the entire sorted story in 2 Samuel 11.

15. Read 2 Samuel 12 for an account of the sufferings and evil brought on because of David's sin. Read Psalms 32, 38, and 51 to get a picture of the guilt and separation from God that David experienced.

must be lowered and valleys filled. St. Francis tells us that the spiritual ditches and valleys are lukewarmness and tepidity. We cover these depressions by filling our hearts with confidence and hope, knowing that "our salvation (Jesus) is near."

The spiritual mountains barring the way are presumption and pride. These, indeed, are great obstacles. Only humility will lower them.

The twisting and crooked paths on the spiritual plain, according to Francis de Sales, are perverse and devious intentions. We straighten the road when our heart is fixed on God—when we only do what pleases Him. St. Francis tells us, "Be like the mariner who, in steering his vessel, always keeps his eye on the needle of the compass; and those who sail their little boats always keep their hands on the tiller."[16]

Embrace the Message

Jesus is the way. He is the answer. He is the prize. The first step toward Him is repenting of anything that is not of Him. That is the core of John's message. He called people to acknowledge their sins, repent, and be baptized. Some procrastinated and missed the grace of the moment. Others could not get past their spiritual avarice and respond to the message. Some were not ready to repent of the sins they kept hidden. Still others got lost in the mountains and valleys of lukewarmness, presumption, or pride. John's message is as relevant today as it was two thousand years ago. It is the message of Advent—a message we need to hear every year. Prepare for the coming of Jesus by a sincere examination of conscience, repentance, the Sacrament of Confession, and doing penance. Don't procrastinate. Don't equivocate. Don't make excuses. Don't rely on old grace. Go to Confession, hear the words of absolution, and be forgiven.

---

16. St. Frances de Sales, *Sermons*, 47.

FOR PERSONAL REFLECTION AND APPLICATION

- Ask the Holy Spirit where He is calling for a response from you. ("*Hodie, nunc!*—Today now.") Prayerfully develop a plan to address this area in your life. Ask for God's grace so that you can follow through on your resolve.

- Read Psalm 32, and reflect on the ill effects of unrepented sin and on the gladness of those who repent and find God's mercy.

JOHN THE BAPTIST
Pointing to Jesus
He Must Increase

❦

God's relationship with man is most amazing. The Divine interacts with the mortal. Eternity impinges on the temporal. The Perfect touches the sinful. Total Love works with those who are not always lovable. The Changeless chooses the fickle. Perfect Holiness dies for the sinful. The All-just accepts the undeserving penitent. God is all-powerful, yet "a bruised reed he will not break, a smoldering wick he will not quench" (Matthew 12:20, NAB). We are nothing without God and all our good is dependent upon His grace and mercy.

There is an even deeper mystery. We, sinful and weak, can have merit and be active partners in God's work. How does God want to reach those who do not know Him or do not acknowledge Him? Certainly, the Holy Spirit is at work, but it is also true—and this is a mind-blowing fact that should give us pause to reflect—God asks His followers, you and me, to introduce Him to other men and women. We can please God. We are able to love Him and our neighbor not only because of His grace but because we are able to choose. Free will makes it possible. God does not overpower us; He invites us. He chooses to work with us and through us in His plan for the restoration of all things in Christ.[1]

That is exactly what John the Baptist did. Recognizing and accepting his vocation as a herald, he used his God-given talents in the service of God. He sought first God's kingdom. He was a witness whose goal was always to introduce others to God. Seeking not his own glory, he desired neither titles nor power. He remained attentive to the leading of the Holy Spirit. John's message was clear and focused. "John testified to [Jesus] and cried out, saying, 'This was he of whom I said, "The one who is coming after me ranks ahead of me because he existed before me"'" (John 1:15, NAB). This was true even before Jesus had begun His public ministry.

When Jesus did arrive publically on the scene, John modified his ministry accordingly.

> [John] saw Jesus coming toward him and said, "Behold, the Lamb of God, who takes away the sin of the world. He is the one of whom I said, 'A man is coming after me who ranks ahead of me because he existed before me.' I did not know him, but the reason why I came baptizing with water was that he might be made known to Israel." John testified further, saying, "I saw the Spirit come down like a dove from the sky and remain upon him. I did not know him, but the one who sent me to baptize with water told me, 'On whomever you see the Spirit come down and remain, he is the one who will baptize with the holy Spirit.' Now I have seen and testified that he is the Son of God."(John 1:29–34, NAB)

John did more than point to Jesus; he sent his disciples to Him. John let it be known that he must—and we must—decrease, and Jesus increase.[2] We read the following concerning two

---

1. See Acts 3:21.
2. See John 3:22–36.

disciples of John the Baptist. "John was there . . . with two of his disciples, and as he watched Jesus walk by, he said, 'Behold, the Lamb of God.' The two disciples heard what he said and followed Jesus" (John 1:35–37, NAB).

St. Francis de Sales, using Sts. Hilary and John Chrysostom as his sources, says that John had three reasons for sending his disciples to Jesus.

First, John wanted everyone to know Jesus as Messiah—personally and intimately. That was the reason for, and focus of, his preaching. That should be our goal as well. Francis de Sales tells us: "We ought neither to seek nor to obtain anything but this: that He . . . be known [by] everyone."

LEARNING FROM THE SOURCE

According to de Sales, the second reason the Baptist sent his followers to Jesus, even though John's public ministry started before that of Jesus, was that Jesus was John's teacher. John wanted his disciples to learn directly from the master Teacher. St. Paul tells us that the entire Old Testament, with all its rules, was a temporary tutor that gave way to Jesus when he arrived.[3] In essence, John was the culmination of the Old Covenant and the last witness pointing to the arrival of the New Covenant.

St. Francis writes:

> John meant: "I am not content to assure you that it is He whom we await. I am sending you that you may be instructed by Him personally. . . ." Teachers . . . were successful only to the degree that they urged and persuaded others to seek out our dear Savior to be instructed by Him personally."[4]

3. See Galatians 3:24–25.
4. St. Francis de Sales, *Sermons*, 6.

De Sales says that pagans and heretics "deliver beautiful, subtle, and finely crafted discourses, whose sole purpose is not to lead souls to Jesus Christ, but only to themselves!"[5]

In our Catholic understanding, we don't go to Mass to hear a great preacher. We go to Mass to encounter Jesus. Within Protestant churches, there is a temptation to foster a cult of personality. People often choose a mega church because of the charismatic preacher and his impressive sermons, or because of the excellent music ministry. Powerful preaching and great music ministry are only worthwhile if they lead us to Jesus.

Cults of personality are dangerous, and even have been seen in certain Catholic ministries. People are sinners and if your faith depends on a human being, you are in a very precarious position. Some Catholic preachers, with large followings, have fallen into sin and people have become disillusioned. Strong charismatic preachers are a blessing, but Jesus must be the center of attention. Recall the Scripture where Jesus tells us that it is better to have a millstone put around the neck and be thrown into the sea rather than to lead one of His little ones astray.[6]

You and I, who have a ministry far less reaching, still need to have the right perspective. Our good example and our testimony to God's work in our personal lives are not to bring accolades to us but to help people meet their Lord and Savior, Jesus.

CORRECT ATTACHMENTS

St. Francis de Sales gives a third reason that John sent his disciples to Jesus. John did not want them to be attached to him, but to Jesus. I find it interesting that John did not just send his disciples to observe Jesus, but he told them to ask Jesus a question. "John summoned two of his disciples and sent them to the Lord to ask, 'Are you the one who is to come, or should we look for another?'" (Luke 7:18–19, NAB). John desired that his followers not merely watch Jesus; he wanted them to interact with Jesus.

---

5. St. Francis de Sales, *Sermons*, 6.
6. See Matthew 18:6, Mark 9:42–48, and Luke 17:1–2.

St. Francis writes,

> St. John sent them to this Divine Majesty to be
> instructed and informed of the truth. . . . He sent
> them for their own benefit and advantage . . . not
> to draw them to himself but to detach from him;
> to let them see the miracles that Jesus Christ per-
> formed."[7]

Consider what follows the Scripture that I quoted earlier.
John the Evangelist writes,

> John was standing with two of his disciples; and
> he looked at Jesus as he walked, and said, "Behold,
> the Lamb of God!" The two disciples heard him
> say this, and they followed Jesus. Jesus turned,
> and saw them following, and said to them, "What
> do you seek?" And they said to him, "Rabbi"
> (which means Teacher), "where are you staying?"
> He said to them, "Come and see." They came and
> saw where he was staying; and they stayed with
> him that day, for it was about the tenth hour. One
> of the two who heard John speak, and followed
> him, was Andrew, Simon Peter's brother. He first
> found his brother Simon, and said to him, "We
> have found the Messiah" (which means Christ).
> (John 1:35–41)

Note that John pointed out Jesus to Andrew, and then
Andrew brought his brother to meet the Lord. A dynamic we
should embrace. Our job as followers of Jesus, as Catholics, and as
evangelists is to introduce Him to others. Only when the individual has a personal relationship with Jesus can the person progress
in the spiritual life. As Catholics we are called to serve people, to

---

7. St. Francis de Sales, *Sermons*, 6.

keep the commandments, to pray, to live good moral lives. All of those things are wonderful and important but they are only means to an end. Our prime call is to know and love our Lord, and then to make Him known and loved.

Perhaps the saddest Scripture is in Matthew 7 where Jesus says,

> Not everyone who says to me, "Lord, Lord," will enter the kingdom of heaven, but only the one who does the will of my Father in heaven. Many will say to me on that day, "Lord, Lord, did we not prophesy in your name? Did we not drive out demons in your name? Did we not do mighty deeds in your name?" Then I will declare to them solemnly, "I never knew you. Depart from me, you evildoers." (vs. 21–23, NAB)

We need to know Jesus personally and help others to know Him personally.

When people ask me to pray or they seek my advice, I am happy to oblige. But I also tell them to pray. I ask them to read Scripture. I give them prayers that they can use (i.e. pray this every day). I do this specifically because they need to develop or deepen a relationship with our Lord, not with me.

FOR PERSONAL REFLECTION AND APPLICATION

- We must be humble if we are to decrease and if Christ is to increase in our lives and in our Christian witness. Consider the Litany of Humility and make it your own prayer.

LITANY OF HUMILITY
by Rafael Cardinal Merry del Val (1865–1930),
Secretary of State for Pope St. Pius X

O Jesus! meek and humble of heart, hear me.
From the desire of being esteemed, *deliver me, Jesus.*

From the desire of being loved . . .
From the desire of being extolled . . .
From the desire of being honored . . .
From the desire of being praised . . .
From the desire of being preferred to others . . .
From the desire of being consulted . . .
From the desire of being approved . . .
From the fear of being humiliated . . .
From the fear of being despised . . .
From the fear of suffering rebukes . . .
From the fear of being calumniated . . .
From the fear of being forgotten . . .
From the fear of being ridiculed . . .
From the fear of being wronged . . .
From the fear of being suspected . . .

That others may be loved more than I, *Jesus, grant me the grace to desire it.*

That others may be esteemed more than I . . .
That, in the opinion of the world, others may increase and I may decrease . . .
That others may be chosen and I set aside . . .
That others may be praised and I unnoticed . . .
That others may be preferred to me in everything . . .
That others may become holier than I, provided that I may become as holy as I should . . .

- I now encourage you to close this book. Draw near to our Lord, speak to him from your heart, and allow Him the opportunity to speak to you. Deepen your relationship with Him.

THE WITNESSES
The Shepherds, the Magi, Simeon, and Anna

FOLLOW *the* EXAMPLE
of the SHEPHERDS
❦

For some camping out at the entrance of Walmart or some other retail store to buy a "door buster" special is a regular pre-Christmas ritual. They wait long hours, in lengthy lines, in bitter cold to get that prized Christmas gift. The Church also has a pre-Christmas ritual. Advent is a time of awaiting the arrival of the most precious of gifts—the Savior who brings us joy, hope, and the promise of eternal life. It is worth waiting and sacrificing for those gifts.

Luke tells us of shepherds who were awake on that first Christmas, "living in the fields and keeping the night watch over their flock" (Luke 2:8, NAB). Their waiting was not a passive activity. On the contrary, they were alert to all danger and ready to protect what was entrusted to them. No wolf or lion could successfully attack while they were on watch.

The job responsibilities of shepherds point us toward spiritual responsibilities of Catholics. During Advent we also need to be awake, alert, and on guard to protect what is entrusted to us.

To understand what it means to be awake and vigilant, let's look at the opposite: three instances of notorious sleepers.

SAMSON

One example is Samson.[1] We are told, "The spirit of the Lord came upon him" (Judges 14:19) and he defended Israel against her enemies. But he began to waver in his vocation. Instead of focusing on the things of God, the lures of sensuality and the pleasures of this world seduced him. His hair, uncut because of his consecration to God, was the symbol of his relationship with the Lord. While he slept in a sinful relationship, Delilah cut his hair, symbolizing the severing of his relationship with God.

The Holy Spirit comes upon each of us at Baptism, bringing us into the family of God. If we are not awake and vigilant, we too can be lulled to sleep by sin. Our relationship with God can be broken or weakened. Instead, following the example of the shepherds, we need to be on our guard, resisting temptation and keeping our focus on our Savior. The time of preparation before Christmas is an opportunity for each of us to ask ourselves, "Have I been sleeping spiritually? Where have I allowed sin to take root in my life?"

DAVID AND SAUL'S GUARDS

We find other notorious sleepers in an incident involving a future king, David, and the reigning king, Saul.[2] As the story of their relationship unfolds, Saul begins to see David as his enemy and seeks to kill him. At a pivotal point in the story, David comes upon the sleeping Saul, who is surrounded by napping guards. David could have easily put an end to the first king of Israel but he stays his hand. He realizes that God had made Saul king and that it would be wrong to take his life. Later, David chides the leader of Saul's guards, "You deserve death because *you have not guarded . . .* the Lord's anointed" (1 Samuel 26:16, emphasis added).

Again, we, like Saul's guards, have been given responsibility to guard that which God has established. In our day and in our culture God's Church and His people are often under siege. Think

---

1. See Judges 13–16.
2. See 1 Samuel 26.

of all the attacks against the dignity of human life and against the Christian understanding of marriage and family. Too many Christians are sleeping on the job, unwilling to oppose the cultural trends of our time and to stand up for God's plan for the world.

We can imitate the vigilance of the shepherds by spending time during Advent, or at any time of the year, getting more acquainted with the reasons why the Church refuses to call homosexual partnering marriage, why assisted suicide can never be justified, why abortion is intrinsically evil, why contraception is disordered, and why capital punishment is problematic.

Christ has entrusted the truth to His Church, of which we are members. As the shepherds guarded what was entrusted to them, we too must guard what has been entrusted to us. Growing in understanding of what the Church teaches is an important step in the right direction.

THE APOSTLES IN THE GARDEN

Perhaps the most notorious sleepers were the Apostles. While Jesus was deep in prayer with His Father—prayer that would change the world—the Apostles were napping. Jesus rebuked them, "Could [you] not keep watch with me for one hour?" (Matthew 26:40).

Advent calls us to prayer: words of love, thanks, and praise to our Lord; requests for strength in overcoming temptations; petitions for our loved ones, for the Church, and for the world. The weeks before Christmas are often busy and tiring, but let us not sleep when we should be praying. God is asking it of us.

How often He is alone. Find time, even if for a few minutes, to regularly stop and visit our Lord in the tabernacle. When I lived in the Boston area there was a Catholic Church near our home. Unfortunately, it was usually locked. I remember kneeling on the steps outside the church. I did so because I knew that our Lord was there on the other side of the door. Jesus tells us, "Knock, and it will be opened to you" (Matthew 7:7). Although my knock would not open the physical door, Jesus opened His heart to mine during those brief visits. Our Lord is always awake and waiting for me. Indeed, our Lord is waiting for all of us.

IMITATING THE SHEPHERDS IN VIGILANCE AND PRAYER

Undoubtedly, the Shepherds were alert and watchful. The Catechism, in speaking of prayer, also speaks of vigilance—not only vigilance from outside enemies but from enemies within the person.

> [T]he battle against the possessive and dominating self requires vigilance, sobriety of heart. When Jesus insists on *vigilance*, he always relates it to himself, to his coming on the last day and every day: *today*. The bridegroom comes in the middle of the night; the light that must not be extinguished is that of faith: "Come," my heart says, "seek his face!" (2730)

The words from the Catechism are a good prayer for Advent or any time of the year: "Your face, Lord, I seek!" (Psalms 27:8, NAB).

THE FRUIT OF VIGILANCE

If we are vigilant, what is the result? For the shepherds heaven opened.

> And an angel of the Lord appeared to them, and the glory of the Lord shone around them, and they were filled with fear. And the angel said to them, "Be not afraid; for behold, I bring you good news of a great joy which will come to all the people; for to you is born this day in the city of David a Savior, who is Christ the Lord. And this will be a sign for you: you will find a babe wrapped

in swaddling cloths and lying in a manger." And suddenly there was with the angel a multitude of the heavenly host praising God and saying,

"Glory to God in the highest,
and on earth peace among men with whom he is pleased!"(Luke 2:9–14)

Those who are vigilant will see God! They will see the "Messiah and Lord" as the angels said. The vigilance of the shepherds gave them a little taste of heaven. To them the heavenly host of angels provided a concert: "Glory to God in the highest and on earth peace to those on whom his favor rests."

Truly, God's favor fell upon those shepherds who were awake, alert, and ready. So, too, it can be for us. We too can taste a bit of heaven, if we strive for holiness and love God during Advent.

SIMPLICITY

There is another virtue possessed by shepherds that is worth noting. Shepherds are simple and humble. They live in a way that the Catechism teaches, "in the simplicity of a life in conformity with the Lord's example, abiding in his truth" (CCC 2470). They are poor in terms of the wealth of the world but rich in the ways of God.

When I think of those shepherds on Christmas morning, some Scriptures come to mind:

- Proverbs 3:34 "When [the Lord] is dealing with the arrogant, he is stern, but to the humble he shows kindness" (NAB). As it was with the shepherds, so it can be with us.
- Matthew 11:25 "Jesus declared, 'I thank you, Father, Lord of heaven and earth, that you have hidden these things from the wise and understanding and revealed them to infants.'"

- Matthew 5:3 "Blessed are the poor in spirit, for theirs is the kingdom of heaven." The kingdom of heaven is our goal and, if we embrace simplicity, childlike trust, humility, and poverty of spirit, heaven will be our home.
- James 4:6–10 "Therefore, it says: 'God resists the proud, but gives grace to the humble.' So submit yourselves to God. Resist the devil, and he will flee from you. Draw near to God, and he will draw near to you. Cleanse your hands, you sinners, and purify your hearts, you of two minds. . . . Humble yourselves before the Lord and he will exalt you" (NAB).

Indeed these Scriptures provide a good summary of Advent preparation and a guide to the entire Christian life:

- Submit to God
- Resist the devil
- Be cleansed and purified

Humble submission to God prepares a person to withstand the storms of life. Shepherds must be prepared for harsh weather and attacks upon the sheep by predators. Because they were expectant and prepared, they were ready to take action. This character trait helped them to respond to God's call.

St. Luke tells us,

> When the angels went away from them into heaven, the shepherds said to one another, "Let us go over to Bethlehem and see this thing that has happened, which the Lord has made known to us." And they went with haste, and found Mary and Joseph, and the baby lying in a manger. (2:15–16).

RAPID RESPONSE

Notice that the shepherds went "with haste." A timely response to God is always appropriate. For example, when the people of Israel sin, Moses "makes haste" to fall on his face to seek forgiveness from God (Exodus 34:8). When Jesus calls Zacchaeus from his perch in a tree, Zacchaeus "made haste and came down, and received [Jesus] joyfully" (Luke 19:6). When Mary heard that her kinswomen Elizabeth was pregnant, "Mary arose and went with haste into the hill country, to a city of Judah, and she entered the house of Zechari'ah and greeted Elizabeth" (Luke 1:39–40).

Whether it is the need for repentance, a call to follow, or the opportunity to serve, running to God is the correct response.

Indeed, for all of us, time is short. Advent is only four weeks. Our earthly life is short. Even with all of our technical and medical advances, the Scripture is still true.

> The years of our life are threescore and ten,
>   or even by reason of strength fourscore;
> yet their span is but toil and trouble;
>   they are soon gone, and we fly away. (Psalms 90:10)

The shepherds also make haste because they are full of joy at the knowledge that the Savior is near. They are eager to see the Promised One. Their joy is so great that they do not hesitate to leave their livelihood behind. What had been their first priority falls to second place. Their action finds a voice in the words of St. Paul.

> But whatever gain I had, I counted as loss for the sake of Christ. Indeed I count everything as loss because of the surpassing worth of knowing Christ Jesus my Lord. For his sake I have suffered the loss of all things, and count them as refuse, in order that I may gain Christ and be found in him, not having a righteousness of my own, based on law, but that which is through faith in Christ, the righteousness from God that depends on faith. (Philippians 3:7–9)

SHEPHERD EVANGELISTS

St. Luke reports, "And when [the shepherds] saw it they made known the saying which had been told them concerning this child; and all who heard it wondered at what the shepherds told them" (Luke 2:17–18).

They who had received the Good News from angels shared it with others. Simple and uneducated shepherds—not theologians—became evangelists after meeting the infant Jesus and His devout mother and foster father. The result of their proclamation was amazement among those who heard it—in fact, among *all* who heard the message. Wonder leads to contemplation and openness to discovery. How many who heard the words of the shepherds drew nearer to God because of it? Only God knows.

Those who were often alone and silent on the hills and plains of Judea sought others and enthusiastically shared what they had the good fortune to behold. If shepherds, who had only seen the birth of the Messiah, can be evangelists, certainly we who know the full story of redemption—Jesus' life, death, Resurrection, Ascension, and sending of the Holy Spirit—have even more good news and reason to share. Moses, Jeremiah, and St. Paul[3] all had compelling reasons why they could not speak for God, but they nonetheless did, and the effects of their proclamation were history changing.

When was the last time you proclaimed the Good News to someone? Good example is important, but words are needed as well. A good question for our reflection is, "What keeps me from witnessing to others?" Then recall the example of the shepherds, trust in the Holy Spirit, and tell someone the Gospel.

Need some suggestions? Invite your family to pray together or suggest you read the Christmas story in the Gospel of Luke and discuss it. When someone tells you about Christmas shopping, tell them of your intention to be at the Christmas Vigil Mass—even better, ask them to join you! Share some insight

---

3. Moses: "Moses said to the LORD, 'Oh, my LORD, I am not eloquent, either heretofore or since you have spoken to your servant; but I am slow of speech and of tongue'" (Ex 4:10). Jeremiah: "Then [Jeremiah] said, 'Ah, Lord God! Behold, I do not know how to speak, for I am only a youth" (Jer 1:6). St. Paul: "I am unskilled in speaking" (2 Cor 11:6).

you've received from this book. Send Christmas cards with a truly Christian message and include a personal note that points toward Jesus. When someone tells you how wearied they are by the pre-Christmas season, ask him or her if you can pray for them. Then do it right there and then (remember that "haste" response of the shepherds!).

THE GOOD SHEPHERD

We are looking at shepherds, not only because of who they are, but also because of whom they point to—Jesus the Good Shepherd who, interestingly, is also the Lamb of God.

They who were shepherding sheep on that early Christmas morning saw in Christ the Shepherd they must follow. They who had authority over sheep placed themselves under the authority of the Good Shepherd. Those shepherds became obedient sheep.

All of us have some authority: parent, grandparent, godparent, employer, teacher, or leader in some organization—even in a group of friends when the question arises as to what to do or where to go for an evening activity. If nowhere else, we have authority over ourselves—we must take responsibility to move in the right direction in this life in anticipation of the life to come. Anyone in authority—again, all of us—are to submit to the leadership and authority of the Good Shepherd and follow His will and plan.

It is a great blessing to be sheep under the care of the Good Shepherd. The author of the Book of Revelation glimpses a heavenly reality and tells us: "For the Lamb who is in the center of the throne will shepherd them and lead them to springs of life-giving water, and God will wipe away every tear from their eyes" (Revelation 7:17, NAB).

The effect of submission to the Good Shepherd is seen nowhere better than in Psalm 23. I'll end this chapter by meditating on it.

- *"The Lord is my shepherd; I shall not want."* God is near to us. We can trust Him as He tells us, "I am the good shepherd. A good shepherd lays down his life for the sheep"

(John 10:11). We have all we need because God became man and died for our salvation. He has opened the gates of heaven and to there He will lead us, if we only will follow.

Take special note of the very personal nature of His care. He is *my* shepherd. He knows my name and calls me by it. Just as an earthly shepherd knows his sheep, Christ knows and loves us personally.

- *"He makes me lie down in green pastures. He leads me beside still waters."* Here note that the psalmist addresses God directly. Our God is approachable. We can speak to Him and He will speak to us.

  St. Augustine states that the green pastures where we can graze are the Word of God. In the pages of the Bible God speaks to us. The same Holy Spirit who inspired the writer can also inspire us the readers.

  St. Augustine also quotes Psalms 119:103 in this same vein, "How sweet to my tongue is your [word], sweeter than honey to my mouth!" That is what we are doing right now, meditating on God's Word and savoring it! A practice we can do in Advent, Christmas, and throughout the year.

- *"He restores my soul. He leads me in paths of righteousness for his name's sake."* We follow the Good Shepherd not only for our benefit; it is *"for the sake of His name."* When we follow the Good Shepherd, we glorify God. We the created are to adore the Creator. We the saved are to extol the Savior. We the sheep are to glorify the Good Shepherd. That only happens when we obediently heed His call and follow Him.

- *"Even though I walk through the valley of the shadow of death, I fear no evil; for you are with me; your rod and you staff, they comfort me."* We have enemies in this life—the world, the flesh, the devil.[4] If we follow the Good Shepherd, we have

---

4. See Mark 4:14–20 for a good description of how these affect the reception of God's word in a person's life. For the devil's activity, see 1 Peter 5:8.

security and a hope that is sure. We will have trials and difficulties but we will not be overwhelmed.

Two Scripture passages from Luke are most helpful. "Do not be afraid any longer, little flock" (12:32, NAB). If we seek His kingdom, as members of the flock, we need not fear. Indeed, "even the hairs of your head have all been counted. Do not be afraid. You are worth more than many sparrows" (12:7, NAB).[5]

The rod and staff are signs of authority. He drives away our enemies and causes the demons to quake; He also leads us in ways of righteousness.

- *"You prepare a table before me in the presence of my enemies; you anoint my head with oil, my cup overflows."* In the seven sacraments God does effective work in those who receive them and seek to respond to the graces given through them. What better food than the Eucharist offered on the altar table in every Catholic Church? Every Mass re-presents the unique sacrifice of Calvary—the willing sacrifice of Jesus that shattered the hold of sin upon us.

  Also, there are four sacraments in which anointing is an important component: Baptism, Confirmation, Anointing of the Sick, and Holy Orders. Moreover, God is not stingy in the grace He gives. He gives in abundance, until our "cup overflows!" (Psalms 23:5).

- *"Surely goodness and mercy shall follow me all the days of my life; and I shall dwell in the house of the Lord for ever."* What a work of mercy and goodness is the Sacrament of Reconciliation! How good God is to give us a sacrament of spiritual healing and strengthening. When we wander, His love can bring us back to the fold. Recall the story of the Prodigal Son.[6] The Father is waiting with open arms to receive his repentant son and to bring him again into the "house of the Lord."

5. This was a favorite quote of Pope St. John Paul II.
6. See Luke 15:11–32.

God pursues us out of love. In following this Shepherd, we have hope of heaven. That is where He is leading us.

CONCLUSION

The shepherds knew their responsibilities. They were alert to the threat of evil; they protected what was entrusted to them; and they looked to the heavens when they heard the call of the angels. (Luke 2:8–14). They received their reward when they saw a newborn Baby who had come to save them and the world. Let's follow the example of the shepherds—alert, faithful, awake, prayerful, and ready for the coming of our Savior.

FOR PERSONAL REFLECTION AND APPLICATION

- Ask God for guidance and then examine yourself. Where have you "fallen asleep" in your life as a disciple of Christ. What practical steps can you take to get back on track? Make a plan and examine your progress, or lack thereof, as part of your every-evening examination of conscience.
- If the shepherds could be evangelists, certainly anyone can. Are you responding to the call to spread the Gospel? Read or reread Pope Francis' Apostolic Exhortation *Evangelii Gaudium* On the Proclamation of the Gospel in Today's World. Find ways you can spread the Good News.

WISE MEN STILL SEEK HIM
Following the Star

"Seek, and you will find" (Matthew 7:7). Jesus spoke those words during what is commonly called the Sermon on the Mount (see Matthew 5–7). Roughly thirty years before Jesus uttered those words, a group of magi was performing them. They sought and found a treasure beyond compare. Matthew preserved this story for us.

> When Jesus was born in Bethlehem of Judea, in the days of King Herod, behold, magi from the east arrived in Jerusalem, saying, "Where is the newborn king of the Jews? We saw his star at its rising and have come to do him homage." (2:1–2, NAB)

Most recent Catholic translations use the term "wise men" to describe these seekers.[1] Who were these men? The *Dictionary of the Bible* tells us that "magi" was a common Greek word to

---

1. See Rheims New Testament; the New Testament translation by Ronald Knox; Revised Standard Version, Catholic Edition; and the Jerusalem Bible. The 1956 translation by James A. Kliest, S.J. uses magi.

designate "a member of the Persian priestly class,"[2] and the term was used to designate those who had special knowledge or power gained through astrology. In a footnote to this passage in a 1956 translation of the New Testament, Father James Kliest notes, "Magi: the term was at the time common throughout the Near East. In general it designated a class of sages or learned men."[3]

There is mystery that shrouds their origin. Matthew only tells us that they came from the East. Some scholars believe they were Zoroastrian priests of the ancient Medes and Persians. However, perhaps it is best we do not know their country of origin. Therefore, they remain international, intercultural, and interreligious. They have a universal message and they accentuate the world-reaching significance of the birth of Jesus. What they teach transcends time, and we don't want to miss their message as we contemplate Advent and Christmas.

In the story of the wise men we see Gentiles responding to the arrival of the Messiah. How did they even know to look for a new king? Paul gives us a hint.

> For what can be known about God is evident . . . because God made it evident. . . . Ever since the creation of the world, his invisible attributes of eternal power and divinity have been able to be understood and perceived in what he has made. (Romans 1:19–20, NAB)

It's fitting that men who studied the cosmos and the wonder of creation would be seeking the Creator. God's existence and His law can be discerned by natural lights and He made us to relate to Him. There is something inside us—something at the core of our being—that pushes us to seek a greater reality.

---

2. John L. McKenzie, S.J., "Magi" in *Dictionary of the Bible* (New York: The MacMillan Company, 1965), 534.

3. James A. Kliest, S.J., *The New Testament Rendered From the Original Greek With Explanatory Notes*, Part One: The Four Gospels (Milwaukee: The Bruce Publishing Company, 1956), 17.

God profoundly revealed Himself to the Israelites, the Jews, in history. They were His chosen people. The birth of Jesus was the beginning of the culmination of God's revelation to them. Yet, when Jesus was born, most of the Jews in Israel missed His arrival. Only a few were ready to see Him for who He was: some shepherds, and later at Christ's Presentation at the temple, Anna and Simeon. Yet the magi—men who were wise—found God by reflecting on God's creation. They saw a star and it led them to Jesus—truly man but also truly God.

It was a great blessing to be born into a Jewish family and then, for males, to be circumcised as the gateway into the covenant relationship with God. So too it is a great blessing to be born into a Catholic family and receive Baptism, the entry into God's family. There is, however, a challenge for an individual, whether Jewish or Catholic, received into the faith as an infant. There is a temptation to take the faith for granted, or for religious practice to become rote, lacking meaning. It's easy to fall prey to the trap of merely going through the motions, perhaps showing exterior signs of piety but with only the shell of faith.

The patriarch Jacob, early in his life, had a similar shortcoming. When he prayed he addressed "the God of my father Abraham and God of my father Isaac."[4] However, after Jacob (renamed "Israel") wrestled with God[5] he spoke of "the God of Israel" (Genesis 33:20, NAB). Jacob moved from living the religion of his ancestors to a personal relationship with God. It is the difference between knowing about a person and knowing the person.

We who are Catholics have access to the fullness of the truth that God gave to His Church and which He preserves throughout time by the activity of the Holy Spirit. We are God's chosen people of the New Testament, as the Jews were in the Old Covenant. However, our faith is to be more than something handed to us. True, we are the inheritors of the greatest blessing, but how often do we take this great gift for granted? Faith must be more. It must be a personal and ongoing encounter with God.

4. See Gen 31:42, 53 and Gen 32:10.
5. See Gen 32:22–31.

When we read the story of the magi, it should convict us of our failings in knowing, loving, and serving God. This story should enflame our desire for God, encourage us to seek Him, and impel us to follow Him. God must be more than the God of my forefathers. He must be my God, my Savior, my hope, my joy, my best friend. If not, we risk our very lives.

I think that the thirteenth chapter in Luke's Gospel is one of the most disturbing sections of Scripture.

> And some one said to [Jesus], "Lord, will those who are saved be few?" And he said to them, "Strive to enter by the narrow door; for many, I tell you, will seek to enter and will not be able. When once the householder has risen up and shut the door, you will begin to stand outside and to knock at the door, saying, 'Lord, open to us.' He will answer you, 'I do not know where you come from.' Then you will begin to say, 'We ate and drank in your presence, and you taught in our streets.' But he will say, 'I tell you, I do not know where you come from; depart from me, all you workers of iniquity!' There you will weep and gnash your teeth, when you see Abraham and Isaac and Jacob and all the prophets in the kingdom of God and you yourselves thrust out. And men will come from east and west, and from north and south, and sit at table in the kingdom of God. And behold, some are last who will be first, and some are first who will be last." (13:23–30)

Most sons of Israel missed the Messiah in their midst. They were the chosen to whom God had revealed Himself and with whom He had made covenant. Like the Israelites at the time of Jesus, God has greatly graced Catholics of today. He has revealed Himself to us profoundly. We have received the sacraments and their graces that fall in super abundance. Yet we put our eternal salvation at risk if we are not growing in our relationship with Him and seeking His kingship over us, as did the magi. How terrible it will be for those, who upon their death, stand before the throne of God and hear those terrible words: "I do not know you."

There is another Scripture containing the words you and I want to hear when we meet Jesus at our particular judgment: "Well done, good and faithful servant. . . . Enter into the joy of your master" (Matthew 25:23).

LET THE WISE MEN TEACH US WISDOM

Let's explore what these wise men from the East can teach us. Luke tells us they saw a star at its rising. There is only one way to see a star. You need to look up! Wise men and women are able to look beyond the many distractions surrounding them and see the heavens. The Psalmist was looking in the right direction.

> When I look at your heavens, the work of your fingers,
> the moon and the stars which you have established;
> what is man that you are mindful of him,
> and the son of man that you care for him?
> Yet you have made him little less than the angels,
> and you have crowned him with glory and honor.
> You have given him dominion over the works of your hands;
> you have put all things under his feet,
> all sheep and oxen,
> and also the beasts of the field,
> the birds of the air, and the fish of the sea,
> whatever passes along the paths of the sea.
> O Lord, our Lord,
> how majestic is thy name in all the earth! (Psalms 8:3–9)

We must cast our gaze to the heavens for that is where our help comes from. "I lift my eyes. . . . From where does my help come? My help comes from the Lord, who made heaven and earth" (Psalms 121:1–2).

One problem is that we have so many distractions, especially during the time before Christmas. The Church gives us Advent as a time of preparation, a time to ready a manger in our hearts—a place to which Jesus can come and reside. Jesus at His birth found the doors locked to Him. Advent is a time to open the door of our heart and welcome our Savior. Will we open to Him? Perhaps even a more fundamental question: Are we even able to hear the knock? For that too requires our attention.

Attention leading to sight comes about only through prayer as we look to and communicate with God, opening our hearts to Him and listening to that still small voice with which He speaks to us.[6] Following the example of the magi, we need to turn our gaze toward Him. How?

REGULAR PRAYER

For a Christian there is no substitute for prayer. It's absolutely necessary if a person is to make progress in faith, hope, and charity. It's also impossible to avoid sin without prayer. The Catechism states:

Prayer is a vital necessity. . . .

> Nothing is equal to prayer; for what is impossible it makes possible, what is difficult, easy. ... For it is impossible, utterly impossible, for the man who prays eagerly and invokes God ceaselessly ever to sin.[7]

> Those who pray are certainly saved; those who do not pray are certainly damned.[8] (CCC 2744)

---

6. See 1 Kings 19:11–13.
7. St. John Chrysostom, *De Anna* 4, 5:PG 54, 666.
8. St. Alphonsus Liguori, *Del gran mezzo della preghiera*.

A thorough exposition on prayer is beyond the scope of this book, but I offer a few points, especially ones we see reflected in the example of the magi. The "Glossary" of the *Catechism of the Catholic Church* gives a succinct definition for prayer.

> The elevation of the mind and heart to God in praise of his glory; a petition made to God for some desired good, or in thanksgiving for a good received, or in intercession for others before God. Through prayer the Christian experiences a communion with God through Christ in the Church.[9]

As the wise men began their journey by raising their eyes to the heavens, so prayer begins by raising one's spiritual eyes to God. In any good conversation, we start by acknowledging the other's presence, clearing our minds of distraction, turning our attention to the other person, and looking at his face. It is only after this preliminary reorientation that we speak. It is no different with the conversation with God that we call prayer.

We start by turning our attention to God and acknowledging His presence with us by a conscious act of the will. We can do that in our own words, spoken or unspoken, or by using a formula prayer. Here is one used to begin prayer in the presence of the Blessed Sacrament.

> My Lord and my God, I firmly believe that you are here, that you see me, that you hear me. I adore you with profound reverence, I ask your pardon for my sins, and the grace to make this time of prayer fruitful.[10]

---

9. See CCC 2559–2565 for a fuller presentation.
10. James Socias, ed., *Handbook of Prayers* (Princeton, NJ: Scepter Publishers, Inc. 1997), 545.

Aim Well!

There is a story of two men walking in the wilderness when they come upon a grizzly bear. One man has a rifle. The bear begins to charge. Seconds seem like hours as the unarmed man waits for the rifle shot. When the bear is almost upon them, there is a bang and the grizzly falls to the ground. The second man anxiously asks the shooter, "What took you so long to fire?" The man with the rifle states, "I had to take aim. I didn't want to miss."

When we pray, we want to take careful "aim." We want to focus on God and God alone. So putting aside distractions is necessary. For some of us that is more difficult than for others. Our ability to focus may also be more difficult when we have a lot on our minds or when we are tired. Nonetheless, we need to make the effort. Sometimes it seems impossible, but we should not despair. God knows our hearts, and if we make a genuine effort, it is good prayer.

Our daily time of prayer needs to be long enough that we reach that point of attention. In the past I told people who did not pray regularly, to set aside ten minutes a day for mental prayer[11] and grow from there. I now tell people to begin with twenty minutes simply because of this need to clear away distractions. For some people, at some times, it may take ten minutes merely to take aim at God. Additionally, prayer is an act of love for God. Even if we struggle and feel nothing during those twenty minutes (or whatever period of time), it is an opportunity to love our Lord. Therefore, we are not wasting time because our effort to pray is itself prayer.

We want to look directly at God. This is the work not of our physical eyes but of our spiritual eyes. (Although a physical object, such as a crucifix, can help us to concentrate.) This involves

---

11. Father Tanquerey, author of *The Spiritual Life: A Treatise on Ascetical and Mystical Theology*, writes, "Mental prayer is a silent intercourse of the soul with God. . . . Every interior act of the mind or of the heart that tends to unite us to God, such as recollection, consideration, reasoning, self-examination, the loving thought of God, contemplation, a longing of the heart for God—all these may be called by the name of mental prayer" (no.510). As of May 2014 the text is available at http://www.ewtn.com/library/SPIRIT/SLIFE5.TXT.

mental prayer, especially what is often called contemplative prayer. The *Catechism of the Catholic Church* describes it as follows:

> What is contemplative prayer? St. Teresa answers: "Contemplative prayer [*oración mental*] in my opinion is nothing else than a close sharing between friends; it means taking time frequently to be alone with him who we know loves us."[12] Contemplative prayer seeks him "whom my soul loves.[13] It is Jesus, and in him, the Father. We seek him, because to desire him is always the beginning of love, and we seek him in that pure faith which causes us to be born of him and to live in him. In this inner prayer we can still meditate, but our attention is fixed on the Lord himself. (2709)

CONSISTENT EFFORT

Those magi following a star had to give consistent effort to stay on track. Again, we find a parallel to the Christian's effort. The Catechism is helpful.

> The choice of the time and duration of the prayer arises from a determined will, revealing the secrets of the heart. One does not undertake contemplative prayer only when one has the time: one makes time for the Lord, with the firm determination not to give up, no matter what trials and dryness one may encounter. One cannot always meditate, but one can always enter into inner prayer, independently of the conditions of health, work, or emotional state. The heart is the place of

---

12. St. Teresa of Jesus, *The Book of Her Life*, 8, 5 in *The Collected Works of St. Teresa of Avila*, trans. K. Kavanaugh, OCD, and O. Rodriguez, OCD (Washington DC: Institute of Carmelite Studies, 1976), I, 67.

13. Song 1:7; cf. 3:14.

this quest and encounter, in poverty and in faith. (2710)

Prayer is a vital part of our ongoing journey in Christ to the Beatific Vision in heaven. To look at the star once would have been insufficient for the magi. Their continued heavenly gaze kept them on the right course. The sight of the star prompted the movement for the next day. After a day's journey, the wise men would again look at the star to get their bearings and adjust their course. This is the method of prayer for the Christian pilgrim.

Although prayer is a conversation between friends, as Teresa of Avila intimates, it is not always easy and it requires effort on our part. The daily raising of their eyes drew the wise men a little closer to the King of kings every day. They made progress. So too will we, if we pray.

Although no substitute for actual prayer, various techniques can help us in prayer.

Set aside time every day for prayer and commit to it. Be faithful to that appointment with God, as you would to meet a friend or family member at a prearranged time. It's also good to have a backup plan in case something interrupts your normal time for prayer. Make prayer a priority. We always find time to eat and nourish our bodies. Find time to pray. Our souls need that nourishment. If you have trouble keeping your prayer time, ask someone close to you, perhaps your spouse, to remind you and be accountable to that person. Finally, the Mass is the best prayer. Focus your attention at Mass and enter into the prayer that takes place at the altar.[14] Go to Mass often—daily, if possible.

We Catholics, like the magi on their journey, are not sprinters in the spiritual life. We know that we are running a marathon of faith. The distance from Persia (Iran) to Bethlehem is over one thousand miles. The wise men needed the virtue of perseverance to reach the goal of seeing the King, who is King over all

---

14. See my booklet *Faith Basics: Discovering the "Awe" of the Mass* (Steubenville, OH: Emmaus Road Publishing 2012).

other kings. We need that same perseverance in our Christian lives. That is one reason we enter into the season of Advent every year. It gives us another opportunity to get closer to Jesus—to become better and more faithful servants. Take to heart this encouragement from Scripture.

> We desire each one of you to show the same earnestness in realizing the full assurance of hope until the end, so that you may not be sluggish, but imitators of those who through faith and patience inherit the promises. (Hebrews 6:11–12)

For Personal Reflection and Application

- Review how you approach and practice prayer. Make this review a prayer by asking God to open your eyes and improve your spiritual vision. Thank our Lord that he meets you whenever you turn to Him. Let Him know your desire to love Him more and to grow in a deeper relationship with Him.

- Perseverance is a virtue in short supply in our culture. We want things now; often we don't want to enter into the struggle that is involved in mastering what is most important. The Catechism tells us that "this tireless fervor [that] can only come from love" is essential for perseverance (2742). Faithful, humble, trusting prayer increases our love of God. Love leads us to perseverance. Perseverance nurtures fervor, increases love, and enriches our prayer. Seek to make this holy cycle grow in your life.

WISE MEN STILL SEEK HIM
An Insecure King

Matthew continues his account of the wise men, telling his readers of their encounter with the insecure King Herod.

> Now when Jesus was born in Bethlehem of Judea in the days of Herod the king, behold, wise men from the East came to Jerusalem, saying, "Where is he who has been born king of the Jews? For we have seen his star in the East, and have come to worship him." When Herod the king heard this, he was troubled, and all Jerusalem with him; and assembling all the chief priests and scribes of the people, he inquired of them where the Christ was to be born. They told him, "In Bethlehem of Judea; for so it is written by the prophet:
>
> > 'And you, O Bethlehem, in the land of Judah, are by no means least among the rulers of Judah; for from you shall come a ruler who will govern my people Israel.'"

> Then Herod summoned the Wise Men secret-
> ly and ascertained from them what time the
> star appeared; and he sent them to Bethle-
> hem, saying, "Go and search diligently for the
> child, and when you have found him bring
> me word, that I too may come and worship
> him." (Matthew 2:1–8)

Herod had no intention of worshiping this new king. Behind Herod's instruction to the magi, there was a sinister objective—to find this new king and eliminate the threat to his own throne. We are rightly horrified. But is Herod's sin so alien to us? We too can be tempted to the sins of Herod—sins that are all too human.

After all, Herod was only looking out for number one. His power, prestige, and self-interest were threatened. It is tempting to cling to and defend what is "mine." It is the syndrome of a spoiled child, who wants everything his way. We can form all types of "logic" to defend what is most dear to us, forgetting that all is a gift from God and that we are only stewards. This pertains not only to our physical possessions but also to our time and our talent. These too are gifts from a gracious God and we are to submit to His plan and direction in their use.

It is telling that Herod didn't go with the magi. He certainly wanted to find this reputed newborn king. Nevertheless, he not only wouldn't seek Jesus to worship Him, he wouldn't actively search for Jesus even to murder Him. Herod was a prisoner in his own private world. Those vices that Herod displayed—especially pride and greed—enslaved him. They enslave us if we are not seeking Jesus.

Herod was a big fish in a small pond and his fear of losing his position and power was devouring him. To preserve his position he killed anyone and everyone that might be a threat, including his wife and two of his sons. He trusted no one. He married ten times in efforts to ease his isolation, but remained friendless and

alone, holding power only by engendering fear. He died an excru-
ciating death, despised by all around him.[1]

There is only one way to avoid falling to the temptations that
plagued Herod. Be like the wise men and seek Jesus. See the call
to conversion as opportunity to embrace the joy of an encounter
with the Savior. God is unchanging. When we get closer to Him,
we are the ones that must change. When we stand in the light of
Christ, we see our sins, failings, and shortcomings. To avoid the
sin of Herod we must welcome the recognition of our sin so that
we can repent. Confession is invaluable in this regard. Let us not
close our hearts to God but open them and find therein what we
most long for—a hope that does not disappoint.

A THREAT OR A FREEDOM?

Like Herod, we too are tempted to see Jesus as a threat, especially when we sense that God is calling us to step outside of our
comfort zone and follow Him. Perhaps it entails an area of sin, or
the call to live more simply, or to give up a friendship or relationship that is not healthy, or to witness to others about your faith, or
perhaps to commit to some corporal or spiritual work of mercy.[2]
Fear, sloth, pride, or greed may hold us back, but at these times
we must remind ourselves that God loves us, that He gives the
grace we will need, and that He is always trustworthy.

Advent and Christmas are opportunities to get in a right
position before God, to acknowledge all the blessings He has
bestowed on us and to give back to Him. In essence, it is the
call to reject the way of Herod and embrace the way of the magi.
That often begins by giving God praise and thanksgiving. Those
prayers put us in a right position, bowing before the Lord. That
attitude prepares our hearts to go forward with God's plan for us

---

1. See Josephus, *Antiquities*, 17, which, as of May 2014, is available at http://penelope.
uchicago.edu/josephus/ant-17.html.

2. The corporal works are: To feed the hungry; to give drink to the thirsty; to clothe the
naked; to shelter the homeless; to visit the sick; to ransom the captive; to bury the dead. The
spiritual works of mercy are: to instruct the ignorant; to counsel the doubtful; to admonish
sinners; to bear wrongs patiently; to forgive offences willingly; to comfort the afflicted; to
pray for the living and the dead.

today, to entrust ourselves to Him and receive a precious gift, a more profound knowledge of, and intimacy with, Jesus.

Also, note that Herod speaks secretly to the magi. He didn't want his subjects and advisors to see his fear. Vulnerability is a prerequisite for any relationship to deepen. In a marriage, self-revelation is needed for a relationship to develop. It makes us feel vulnerable, and therefore, it is frightening. Yet the opportunity to grow closer to the other requires openness—leaving the shadows of secrecy and coming to the light. Our relationship with God is much the same. Placing ourselves in His hands and entrusting ourselves to Him can be frightening, but ultimately it is freeing.

WHICH WAY?

How many jokes are there about the reluctance of men to ask for directions? This was not a failing of the magi. As they followed the star, there came a point at which they could no longer discern the route forward. They were humble enough to ask for help. Herod had evil on his mind, but the magi acted correctly. They sought assistance when they needed it. We require help to keep on the right path and should seek guidance. Our clouded thinking and disordered passions need to be counterbalanced. We can find direction through the teachings of the Church, by good spiritual and doctrinal reading,[3] and by asking the advice of a confessor, spiritual director, or someone more mature in the faith. That you are reading this book is a testimony to your desire to follow the example of the magi in finding help to stay on the right path.

The magi did receive important information when they sought help, even though the provider was a brutal, self-centered tyrant. Although we should seek direction from godly sources, we should not underestimate God's ability to further His plan and bless His people even through the most unlikely sources. God can and does use the ungodly to forward His plan. For example, Jacob's sons sold their brother, Joseph, into slavery.[4] Despite many trials and

---

3. Check this website for a list of valuable Catholic books: http://www.catholicity.com/mccloskey/readingplan.html (Website available as of June 2014).
4. Read the entire account in Genesis 35–36 and 42–45.

difficulties, God protected and guided Joseph, and eventually reunited him with his brothers. They feared Joseph would exact revenge, yet while admitting their evil intentions in selling him into slavery, Joseph acknowledged God's sovereignty. Joseph said, "As for you, you meant evil against me; but God meant it for good" (Genesis 50:20). God's divine plan cannot be thwarted and He can work good for us in all circumstances. Indeed, "We know that in everything God works for good with those who love him, who are called according to his purpose" (Romans 8:28).

With new clarity, the Scriptures tells us, the magi again saw the star, and they took up their journey with renewed vigor.

FINDING HE WHOM WE SEEK

Matthew continues his account,

> After their audience with the king they set out. And behold, the star that they had seen at its rising preceded them, until it came and stopped over the place where the child was. They were overjoyed at seeing the star. (Matthew 2: 9–10, NAB)

As the star was the reference point in the sky for the magi, Jesus, who is the brightest star in the heavenly realm, must be our reference point. The star helped the wise men keep their bearings. It illuminated their path. Jesus will help us to stay on the right path.

Look to Him at the beginning of your day. Start with a morning offering. Tell Him that you desire to see and follow Him and that you seek unity with Him. Then throughout the day, recall your morning prayer and rededicate your day. Before beginning a task, ask for His guidance. I often recall the words of the blind man who, when asked by Jesus what he desired, responded, "*Domine, ut videam*—Lord, that I may see" (Mark 10:46–52). When I say those words, my prayer is: "Yes Lord, help me to see where you would lead and direct me. Surely, I can be blind to my faults and shortcomings, and without understanding unless you turn on the light."

End each day with prayer. Thank Him for the light and grace He has given you on that day. Confess to Him your sins. Ask His forgiveness. Renew your resolutions. Then fall to sleep with the peace that a child has in the arms of her mother.

In this way we frame our day with prayer, starting and ending with reference to Him who is the alpha and the omega. Also, take opportunities throughout the day to turn a loving glance at Him. It was the approach of the magi and it led them to their goal of seeing God.

JOY AND MORE JOY

The Scripture tells us that these wise men were "overjoyed at seeing the star again." As we said earlier in discussing the infant John the Baptist, followers of Jesus should be marked with joy. We are not lost—no matter what the circumstances. There is a star in the sky, Jesus, to guide us. Even in the face of difficulties, we should continue to experience joy. After all, Jesus loves us and works for our good in all situations.

The faithfulness of the magi pays off. They are elated when they enter the home of the child King. "And going into the house they saw the child with Mary his mother, and they fell down and worshiped him" (Matthew 2:11).

What awe they must have felt to behold the humble abode. What thankfulness they must have experienced upon reaching the goal of their quest. How God's grace must have filled their spirits with joy. Did they dare to touch or even hold the Christ child? How blessed to be able to draw close to the most holy Virgin, who yet was mother. Their journey was worthwhile; they found Him whom they sought—the One who had been their guide.

FOR PERSONAL REFLECTION AND APPLICATION

- Examine yourself. Have you fallen into the sin of Herod? Is there an area in your life that you are reluctant to submit to the Lordship of Christ? Is it due to fear of what God might expect of you? Consider discussing the matter with your confessor, a trusted Christian friend, or a spouse or parent. Find encouragement in the following Scripture, "I, the Lord your God, hold your right hand; it is I who say to you, 'Fear not, I will help you'" (Isaiah 41:13).

- Put yourself in the story of the magi upon finding Jesus. Reflect. When have you felt closest to your Savior? What joy will you experience if you seek Jesus during Advent? Will you join with the angels in their chorus at Christmas? "Glory to God in the highest and on earth peace to those on whom his favor rests" (Luke 2:14, NAB).

WISE MEN STILL SEEK HIM
The Gifts

The magi did not come empty handed to see the King. "And going into the house they saw the child with Mary his mother, and they fell down and worshiped him. Then, opening their treasures, they offered him gifts, gold and frankincense and myrrh" (Matthew 2:11). Their belief in the unique royalty of the One they sought caused them to bring items that they did not personally need for their journey, but which were entirely appropriate for falling in homage before a king. Gold, the most precious metal, honored His status. Frankincense pointed to His position as not only king but also a great high priest, who mediated between God and man. Lastly, they gave myrrh to this child.

The uses of myrrh, a costly ointment in the ancient world, included perfume, medication, and an embalming component. Myrrh, mentioned only three times in the Gospels, foreshadows Christ's death. Mark tells us that the Roman soldiers offered myrrh to Jesus during His crucifixion to ease His pain. "They offered him wine mingled with myrrh; but he did not take it" (Mark 15:23). What He accepted as a child, He rejected from the Cross. He accepted nothing during his Passion that would lessen the offering He gave on our behalf and in obedience to His Father. After His death, we find the third mention of myrrh. Before His burial, some of His followers bound the body of Jesus in a linen cloth and placed it in the tomb. As John the Evangelist explains.

> Nicodemus . . . came bringing a mixture of myrrh and aloes, about a hundred pounds' weight. They took the body of Jesus, and bound it in linen cloths with the spices, as is the burial custom of the Jews. (John 19:39–40)

Nicodemus, a secret follower of Jesus, found courage at His death to honor the One who died for his and our salvation.

Can we bring gifts of similar value to Jesus? Indeed, we can!

GOLDEN GIFTS WORTHY OF THE KING

What gift of gold can we give to our King? Time, talents, and treasure. For many people time seems to be in short supply and is therefore valuable. How we use our time bespeaks of our priorities in life. How much time do I give to prayer? How much time do I give to growing in the faith? How much time in service? The answer to these questions points to our priorities. The scriptural injunction is "seek first his kingdom and his righteousness, and all these things shall be yours as well" (Matthew 6:33).

Talent is another gold standard. Do I recognize my abilities as gifts from God? Do I recall that, as in the parable of the talents, I am to use my gifts in God's service and give Him a return on His investment in me?[1] Do I work conscientiously serving God and not merely men?

We can also use our material riches as a gift of gold to Jesus. "No one can serve two masters; for either he will hate the one and love the other, or he will be devoted to the one and despise the other. You cannot serve God and mammon" (Matthew 6:24). So,

---

1. See Matthew 25:14–30.

do I contribute to the Church? Do I give alms to the poor? Could I use part of my Christmas budget to bless those in want?

Advent is a time to reflect on what "gold"—time, talent, and treasures—I have and how I can make a gift to the King of kings who was born in a stable and died for me. Of course, when we give our gold, we are only returning to God what He has first given to us.

FRANKINCENSE

The next gift is frankincense, which, I believe, represents a greater gift than gold. Incense is associated with prayer, in particular with worship. The gift of gold returns to God what He has given to us. Worship originates within us and, therefore, is of greater value. It is the duty of the created to the Creator and of the saved to the Savior. The author of the Book of Revelation makes the connection between incense and prayer.

> Another angel came and stood at the altar, holding a gold censer. He was given a great quantity of incense to offer, along with the prayers of all the holy ones, on the gold altar that was before the throne. The smoke of the incense along with the prayers of the holy ones went up before God from the hand of the angel. (Revelation 8:3–4, NAB)

The angels are always in God's presence giving him praise, adoration, and worship. If we want to give the Lord the gift of frankincense, we need to join the angel chorus and worship Him. Many of us are most comfortable with prayers of intercession, but worship is the prayer we owe to the good God. It is the style of prayer that, as we gaze upon the Christ child, should well up in our hearts and our minds.

How do we pray in praise? Many of the Psalms will help us, as well as hymns such as "Praise God from Whom All Blessings

Flow" and "A mighty Fortress Is our God," and prayers, such as the *Te Deum*,

> O God, we praise Thee, and acknowledge Thee to be the supreme Lord.
> Everlasting Father, all the earth worships Thee.
> All the Angels, the heavens and all angelic powers,
> All the Cherubim and Seraphim, continuously cry to Thee:
> Holy, Holy, Holy, Lord God of Hosts!
> Heaven and earth are full of the Majesty of Thy glory. . . .

Also, to quiet your spirit and look with love upon Jesus represented in the figure of the Babe in the manger is praise. Words aren't even necessary, only the love that gives the impetus to words. Prayer is first a movement of our spirit. To desire to love and to worship, is to begin to love and worship.

Advent and Christmas are times to offer the frankincense of praise, adoration, and worship to our Lord.

MYRRH

To recap, gold (time, talent, treasure) is a good gift. Frankincense (praise, thanksgiving, worship), although it represents a duty, is a better gift. Myrrh, however, represents the best gift we can give to God.

As mentioned above, myrrh is associated with death, and death is a requirement for true self-giving love. "Greater love has no man than this, that a man lay down his life for his friends" (John 15:13). The death of Jesus on our behalf is the greatest expression of love. He voluntarily gave His life for our salvation.[2]

How do we respond to His great act of love? How do we answer Jesus when He asks, "Do you love me?"[3] We die to self

---

2. See 1 John 3:16, Romans 5:8, 1 Peter 3:18, and Galatians 1:3–4.
3. See John 21:15–19.

and live in and for Christ.[4] In choosing this death, we give the gift of myrrh.

FREEWILL

A gift of God makes this sacrifice of myrrh possible. God has given us freewill, which enables us to love, not as something counterfeit or as the relationship of a pet with its owner. No, we can *truly love*. Because I have freewill, I can choose to do the loving thing.

Because I have freewill I can say "no" to selfishness and "yes" to charity. Martyrs die because their love for God is stronger than their desire to live. There are also many opportunities in our daily life to love by smaller deaths, such as obedience to God in great and small matters, docility to the teaching authority of the Church, loving my neighbor with the love of Christ, acts of mortification freely offered to Christ, and prayer.

ON EASTER MORNING

As mentioned previously, myrrh is a fragrant ointment used to anoint the body of the deceased. On Easter morning some women, who were followers of Jesus, brought spices to His tomb, which probably included myrrh.

> When the sabbath was past, Mary Mag´dalene, and Mary the mother of James, and Salo´me, bought spices, so that they might go and anoint him. And very early on the first day of the week they went to the tomb when the sun had risen. (Mark 16:1–2)

What impelled these women to rise early in the morning only two days after the exhaustion they must have felt as witnesses to the brutal crucifixion of Jesus? They brought spices to anoint the

4. See Luke 9:23; Romans 12:1; Galatians 2:20, and 5:24.

body while not knowing how they would move the heavy stone. The Apostles were hiding in fear of persecution, incarceration, or perhaps death; yet these women overcame that fear. They did not yet comprehend that Christ was to rise, even though He had intimated such on several occasions. Only great love could have moved these women to do what, otherwise, would be considered senseless and reckless. They were willing to die to self in hopes of doing some good on Christ's behalf. The reward for their love—a reward which they did not seek—was to be among the first to witness the Resurrection.

We are to follow the examples of Jesus and of these women. We can decide to die. That is the gift of myrrh we can offer to God. Consider what Paul writes in Ephesians 5:2, "walk in love, as Christ loved us and gave himself up for us, a *fragrant offering* and sacrifice to God."

The myrrh—the holy ointment—that we can offer to the One who gave His life for us, is to follow His example. Use our freewill to choose to die to self and live for Christ and to respond to His love with love! "For Christ I live. For Christ I die."[5] "True love . . . implies a readiness for heroic self-surrender."[6]

Consider what we say in the Our Father. "*Thy* will be done." If we act upon what we pray, we are using our freewill to choose God's will, not our own.

What myrrh (dying to self and living for Christ) can we offer during Advent? We find the answer in the Scripture, in the teaching of the Church, and in the words the Holy Spirit whispers to you and me when we come before God in prayer. Find the answer by going to our Lord and asking Him. Moreover, although love does not seek a return, we do know God will not be outdone in generosity and that all love is but a small reflection of the love of Christ.

Indeed, wise men and women still seek Him! Jesus invites us to come into His presence every day. We don't need a star to guide

---

5. I found this on a t-shirt. See Phil 1:21.
6. Dietrich Von Hildebrand, *Transformation in Christ* (San Francisco: Ignatius Press, 2001), 411.

us. He dwells in us and in those we meet; He is present in His Scriptures; He is most powerfully present in the Eucharist. Every Advent He invites us again. Let's turn to Him willingly and often. Let us bring to Him our gifts for His honor.

FOR PERSONAL REFLECTION AND APPLICATION

- Consider each of the gifts and decide how, in practical ways, you will honor and love God.
- Use my prayer below or your own words and tell our Lord that you love Him.

With joy and gladness, I cry out to You, Lord. Open my heart to sing Your praise, and announce Your goodness and truth. Inspired by the example of the magi, I desire to draw closer to You during the holy seasons of Advent and Christmas. I open my heart and my mind, and I freely choose to give You the gift of my love and of my very self. May everything I think, do, and say give glory to You. Relying on your grace and mercy, I pray in the name of the Father, and of the Son, and of the Holy Spirit. Amen.

AT THE PRESENTATION
Anna and Simeon
❧

The feast of the Presentation of the Lord, celebrated on February second, ends the Christmas season. It is fitting that we end our survey of the characters of Advent and Christmas by reflecting on Anna and Simeon, who speak to us from the Gospel on that feast day.

Mary, Joseph, and the infant Jesus go to the temple in Jerusalem to fulfill the requirements of the Mosaic law.

> And when the time came for their purification according to the law of Moses, they brought [Jesus] up to Jerusalem to present him to the Lord (as it is written in the law of the Lord, "Every male that opens the womb shall be called holy to the Lord") and to offer a sacrifice according to what is said in the law of the Lord, "a pair of turtledoves, or two young pigeons." (Luke 2:21–24)

It is worth noting that Mary and Joseph gave the offering stipulated for the poor. Not only did God stoop to become a man,[1] He chose a humble couple of meager means for his earthly family. Yet, as they presented the offering of the poor, they brought the true wealth of mankind into the temple—the eternal Son of God become Man.

ANNA

While in the temple an elderly woman approached Jesus, Mary, and Joseph.

> There was a prophetess, Anna, the daughter of Phan´u-el, of the tribe of Asher; she was of a great age, having lived with her husband seven years from her virginity, and as a widow till she was eighty-four. She did not depart from the temple, worshiping with fasting and prayer night and day. And coming up at that very hour she gave thanks to God, and spoke of him to all who were looking for the redemption of Jerusalem. (Luke 2:36–38)

Anna recognized Jesus! The temple was the busiest place in the very busy city of Jerusalem. We might compare it to a bustling shopping mall. Hundreds, perhaps thousands, of people were at the temple when Jesus was there. The Second Person of the Trinity was in plain sight, yet the vast majority of people just walked on by. But an eighty-four-year-old widow identified Him.

How was it that Anna recognized Jesus, even as a baby? Her entire life had been a preparation to recognize Him. Luke tells us that, over a long span of time, she "worshiped night and day with fasting and prayer" in the temple.

---

1. See Philippians 2:6–7.

FASTING

We have, in a prior chapter, spoken of the value and necessity of prayer. Fasting also has great spiritual benefit. We can fast from foods or from certain activities—giving up of something good for something better. When we fast by skipping dessert, a snack, an entire meal, a favorite television program, or the Internet for a day, we do it to tell God and ourselves that there is something—actually, someone—more important in life.

Love always involves a certain relinquishment. Jesus sets the example; His life was a sacrifice for us. From the Incarnation to the crucifixion, He demonstrated His love by renunciation of His divine rights. How can we respond to His love? One way is to embrace sacrifices, small or large, as a way to reciprocate. He accepts them as signs of our love, and in uniting our sacrifices to His, we share in His love for mankind.

We know this truth from our earthly life. If I love my wife, I'm more concerned about her well-being than I am about my own. That is why acts of courtesy are so important. To hold the door for my wife is a small gesture but it says to me, and to her, that I am willing to inconvenience myself because I love her.

Most fasts are humble expressions by which I remind myself, and tell God, that He is the one I love and that I willingly embrace these mortifications because of that love.

Worship, prayer, and fasting were the keys to Anna's ability to recognize her Lord. Like a mom who can pick out her child in a hospital nursery, Anna had no trouble recognizing the Messiah. She had been looking toward Him with loving eyes for her eighty-four-year life. Love opens the eyes to see the beloved. Anna's spiritual eyes were well trained.

HELPING OTHERS TO MEET THE BELOVED

Like the shepherds who had previously recognized and proclaimed Jesus, Anna became an evangelist. She "spoke of him to all who were looking for the redemption of Jerusalem" (Luke 2:38). The Navarre Bible Commentary notes,

Everyone who, like . . . Anna, perseveres in piety and in service of God, no matter how insignificant their lives seem in men's eyes, becomes an instrument the Holy Spirit uses to make Christ known to others. In his plan of redemption God avails of these simple souls to do much good to all mankind.[2]

Anna recognized the Christ but she was not the only one in the temple that day who was thrilled to see the promised Messiah.

SIMEON

Luke tells us,

There was a man in Jerusalem, whose name was Simeon, and this man was righteous and devout, looking for the consolation of Israel, and the Holy Spirit was upon him. And it had been revealed to him by the Holy Spirit that he should not see death before he had seen the Lord's Christ. And inspired by the Spirit he came into the temple; and when the parents brought in the child Jesus, . . . he took him up in his arms and blessed God and said,

> Lord, now let your servant depart in peace, according to your word;
> for mine eyes have seen your salvation
> which you have prepared in the presence of all peoples,
> a light for revelation to the Gentiles,
> and for glory to your people Israel.
> (Luke 2:25–32)

2. José María Casciaro, *The Navarre Bible: Saint Luke's Gospel*, 59.

Simeon is one of my favorite New Testament characters. He is an older man, a designation that now applies to me. He was attentive to the Holy Spirit and, although I fall far short of Simeon's attentiveness, I too aspire to it. A little later in the chapter I'll reveal the third reason that I see Simeon as a patron.

ATTENTIVE TO THE HOLY SPIRIT

Three times in as many verses Luke tells us the Holy Spirit was with Simeon. The Holy Spirit was "upon him," "revealed" to him God's plan, and "inspired" Simeon to act. The Third Person of the Blessed Trinity is not a shouter. He usually speaks to us in a whisper. Do you remember the story of Elijah? He was waiting to hear God.

> The Lord . . . said, "Go forth, and stand upon the mount before the Lord." And behold, the Lord passed by, and a great and strong wind rent the mountains, and broke in pieces the rocks before the Lord, but the Lord was not in the wind; and after the wind an earthquake, but the Lord was not in the earthquake; and after the earthquake a fire, but the Lord was not in the fire; and after the fire a still small voice. And when Eli′jah heard it, he wrapped his face in his mantle and went out and stood at the entrance of the cave. And behold, there came a voice to him, and said, "What are you doing here, Eli′jah?" (1 Kings 19:9, 11–13)

Elijah heard God because he patiently listened. Simeon recognized the Messiah because of his devout attention to the Holy Spirit. Both men had spiritually attuned ears. On several occasions in the Gospel, while teaching, Jesus said, "Let him who has ears to hear, hear."[3] It is very possible to have ears that don't hear.

---

3. See Matthew 11:15, Mark 4:9, and Matthew 13:9. See also Revelation 2:7. "He who has an ear, let him hear what the Spirit says to the churches."

All of us probably know someone whom we would identify as insensitive. That type of person doesn't even know when they offend someone. I hope you also know some sensitive people, who are attuned to others and pick up verbal and nonverbal clues. Simeon was sensitive to the Holy Spirit; he was able to hear that "tiny whispering sound." We also need to develop our sensitivity to the Holy Spirit, ask Him to speak to us and guide us, and then listen expectantly.

DYING IN PEACE

While holding the infant Jesus in his arms, Simeon prays, "Lord, now let your servant depart in peace." This verse is my third reason for appreciating Simeon. I have made his prayer my own. I don't want to die until I've accomplished what God has intended for me—until I've finished the work He has given me to do in this life.

My dad was an example to me in this regard. He had seven children and asked God to allow him to see all of his children settled in life. In other words, he wanted to fulfill the work of a father that had been entrusted to him. He died one month after walking his youngest daughter down the church aisle. With all seven of his children married and on their own, he was able to say with Simeon, "Lord, now let your servant depart in peace, according to your word; for mine eyes have seen your salvation."

After I've finished the last task that God has assigned to me, I want to die. I don't want to delay getting to the place where we all want to be—heaven, in the presence of God. I also don't want to leave any earlier.

A PROPHET

After his prayer (Luke 2:29–32), Simeon speaks to Mary,

> Behold, this child is set for the fall and rising of many in Israel,

and for a sign that is spoken against
(and a sword will pierce through your own soul
also),
that thoughts out of many hearts may be revealed.
(Luke 2:34–36)

Simeon spoke prophetically. The Holy Spirit communicated God's word to Mary, and Simeon was a perfect conduit. Mary would cherish and reflect upon those words throughout her life. I think that was the last task that God wanted old Simeon to do on this earth—deliver that message to Mary. We are not told how long he lived after this prophecy, but he was ready to meet his Creator.

FOR PERSONAL REFLECTION AND APPLICATION
- Consider the quote from the Navarre Bible Commentary that I mentioned above in our discussion of Anna. "Everyone who, like Simeon and Anna, perseveres in piety and in service of God, no matter how insignificant their lives seem in men's eyes, becomes an instrument the Holy Spirit uses to make Christ known to others." What impact are you making for the Gospel? Are you yielding to the Holy Spirit? Are you persevering in piety and service? If you are falling short, repent, rededicate yourself, and make a plan to start today.
- Consider that God has a unique plan for you in this life. Tell God you are willing to follow the Holy Spirit wherever He may lead you. Ask for His grace. Spend some quiet, prayerful time listening to God's voice.

CONCLUSION

There is much to learn about ourselves and about God through contemplation of the Incarnation. There is also much to encourage us in the seasons of Advent and Christmas and in the characters that played a part in the preparation and epiphany of the Messiah. I have only scratched the surface of the depth of the love of God. For indeed,

> The Word became flesh for us *in order to save us by reconciling us with God.* . . .
>
> The Word became flesh *so that thus we might know God's love.* . . .
>
> The Word became flesh *to be our model of holiness.* . . .
>
> The Word became flesh to make us *"partakers of the divine nature"* (2 Peter 1:4).
>
> (CCC 457–460, emphasis in the original)

If I have been successful in these reflections, you have found opportunity and impetus for prayer. I wish to end with that same goal. I leave you with a prayer that I wrote long ago and which has helped me through many Advents and Christmases. I pray that it will bless you as well.

A Christmas Prayer

Lord, I desire
to be like Mary and say yes to Your life in me;
to be like the manger, ready to receive You;
to be like the angels, proclaiming Your Good News and singing Your praises;
to be like the shepherds and come to worship You;
to be like the magi and go to whatever distance is necessary to be in Your presence;
to be like John the Baptist giving voice to the need of conversion;
to be like Anna and recognize Your coming in the midst of my way;
to be like Simeon and not see Death until the work You desire in my life has come to fulfillment.
May it be so. Amen.

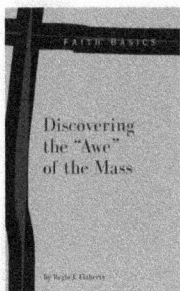

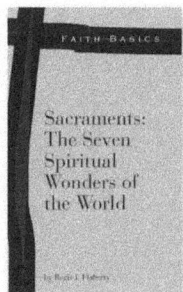

Get to know your . . .

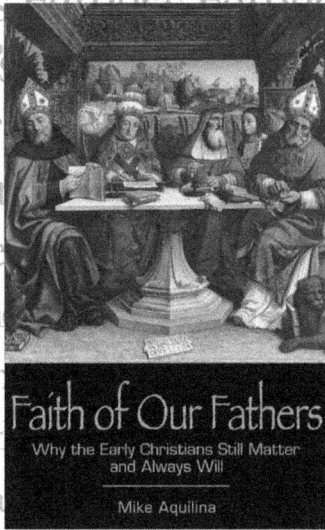

Marriage & Family Life

The Catholic for a Reason series brings together the expert knowledge and personal insight of today's top Catholic apologists on topics at the heart of the Catholic faith. Whether you're a non-Catholic who wants to learn about the Church's teaching, or a Catholic who wants to become a more articulate defender of the faith, the Catholic for a Reason series is for you.

Catholic for a Reason IV

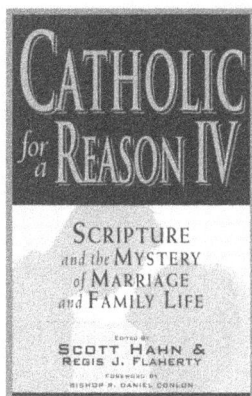

Marriage and family life lived according to God's plan can change lives and change the world! Catholic for a Reason IV explores the Scriptural basis for the Catholic understanding of marriage.

The volume is replete with solid Catholic theology and idealism. . . . While reaffirming the natural law, the authors also sketch out the unique qualities of Christian, sacramental marriage. They cite frequently the teachings of the Second Vatican Council and recent popes, especially John Paul II. . . . Scripture and the Mystery of Marriage and Family Life is not all theology, however. In fact, it is filled with the concrete experiences of married couples who strive to live out their vocation day by day with God's help. Many of their examples of marriage and family life are touching—and very real.

978-1-931018-44-9; $15.95

Join Scott and Kimberly Hahn, Mike Aquilina, and ten other well-known Catholic authors, who along with their spouses, present solid Biblical testimony to the joys, struggles, and sanctity found in the sacrament of Marriage. Essays include "The World as Wedding," "Lessons Learned at Nazareth," and "Reflections on Pope Benedict XVI's First Encyclical."